HOPE FOR A WIDOW'S SHATTERED WORLD

Amy,

    This book is the best I have read for women that have had the world shattered by the loss of their husband. I pray it helps you as you go through your journey of grief.

    In Christ,
    Betty Hodges
    ZUMC Stephen Minister

HOPE FOR A WIDOW'S SHATTERED WORLD

✦

Rebuilding Life Out of the Ashes of Grief

Patsy Brundige and Pat Millican

iUniverse, Inc.
New York Lincoln Shanghai

HOPE FOR A WIDOW'S SHATTERED WORLD
Rebuilding Life Out of the Ashes of Grief

iUniverse books may be ordered through booksellers or by contacting:

iUniverse
2021 Pine Lake Road, Suite 100
Lincoln, NE 68512
www.iuniverse.com
1-800-Authors (1-800-288-4677)

Unless otherwise indicated, Bible quotations are taken from the New Revised Standard Version of the Bible, Copyright 1989, Division of Christian Education of the National Council of Churches of Christ in the United States of America.

ISBN-13: 978-0-595-27460-4

ISBN-10: 0-595-27460-9

Printed in the United States of America

To
Our families who loved us and sustained us through many difficult days.

You have turned my mourning into dancing:
You have taken off my sackcloth
and clothed me with joy,
so that my soul may praise you
and not be silent.
O Lord my God, I will give thanks to you forever.

Psalm 30:11-12

Contents

Part III   RE-DISCOVERING JOY

Part IV   *LIVING IN CONTENTMENT*

ACKNOWLEDGMENTS

We are grateful for the many widows who shared their stories with us. We also appreciate our friends who encouraged us, read and re-read our manuscript, and offered helpful criticism.

FOREWORD

When Patsy Brundige told me she and her friend, Pat Millican, were in the process of writing a book on widowhood, I gave an immediate word of encouragement. I knew they both were widows: one for several years, the other relatively recently. I thought the difference in time periods would provide a depth of perspective. I also was excited about the project, because I knew from personal experience that Patsy was a skillful and creative writer. Pat, I soon learned, was a talented book-reviewer and the designated researcher for all literature in the field of widowhood.

What came as a surprise was their early disclosure to me that though there were many books on the process of grief, few had been written on the unique challenges and nuances of widowhood. After reading their rough draft, I was convinced that they had written and compiled an insightful and poignant book that would offer practical help to widows seeking to put their lives back together. The book itself presupposes a power that comes from beyond, as well as a spiritual core within, and it offers such a faith position with a scarcity of dogma, religious language, or preachy style.

Let me simply say that apart from the insights to be gained from either scanning or devouring these pages, perhaps the greatest comfort it offers is that this journey is not intended to be made alone. Once widows learn that others have experienced strange and unwelcome feelings, thoughts, and behaviors, there is comfort in knowing that one is not on the edge of either insanity or futility—just in the midst of chaos and on the cutting edge of a new, if not frightening, frontier.

There is no short-cut in the process of grief or in the living out of widowhood. The best anyone can offer is wise counsel, loving support, and heart-felt sharing. This book becomes a catalyst for reflection, a glossary of insights, and an early glimmer of hope.

It is with these hopes that I offer my endorsement of this book and wish well to all who open its cover, seeking genuine insights and wise counsel. Let the journey begin.

Dr. Justin Tull
Pastor, Oak Lawn United Methodist Church, Dallas, Texas

PREFACE

We sat together at the lake. Sky and water shared the same grayness. Wind slammed waves against the shore. Bare-branched trees formed dark silhouettes. The grayness was broken only by the explosion of blooms on a redbud tree.

We talked about our children, then slowly we began to share the grayness of our lives. We were linked by decades of friendship, but now more closely than ever by our shared widowhood. Seven years of singleness for one of us, less than a year for the other.

"When does the pain stop? Does it ever really go away? Will healing ever come?"

Her questions hung in the air, gathering the chill of an early spring afternoon.

"Yes, the pain does go away. Completely? Not for a long time. Healing doesn't just 'come,' we work for it; we discover it, at first in tiny happenings tucked in ordinary days."

The rising wind ruffled the lake with whitecaps. We began to gather chairs and cushions. One more question was hardly more than a whisper: "How can I face the future—alone?"

"One step at a time."

MY STORY: PATSY BRUNDIGE

My husband died seven years ago. We were parents of two college-age sons, and I was a United Methodist pastor, serving a large city church. Virgil was a research engineer for a major energy company, traveling all over the world.

Our lives were incredibly busy, but we had settled into a satisfying routine. Virgil looked forward to long weekends on his farm while I was busy with church activities. We treasured moments of family togetherness, snatched from weeks and months of professional partings.

Virgil flew home from a business trip, collapsing in pain. The supposed gall bladder attack was actually cancer of the lung, which claimed his life five months later. During his illness, he never questioned his doctors or mentioned death, thus locking our family in a heart-wrenching game of denial.

He endured massive chemotherapy and radiation treatments, most of which were administered in the hospital where he died. I had left his bedside to prepare for a parishioner's funeral only an hour before his death.

My life would stand still for only one week, as my responsibilities at the church demanded my return. In less than two months, our younger son received his master's degree in architecture; our family was thrust into the long-planned prenuptial parties preceding his wedding; and I was ordained an elder in the United Methodist Church. I moved, zombie-like, through these three life-changing events, compressed into such a short period of time.

Nonetheless, I was sustained by faith in God, whom I felt grieved with me, and by my sons and new daughter-in-law, who lived nearby. My lifeline also included a small, but intimate, circle of longtime friends, and a large, compassionate church family.

MY STORY: PAT MILLICAN

My husband died less than a year ago. At the time of his death, Dick was a geologist who managed an oil and gas division of a large corporation. Our daughter and son were both married. We had one grandson and one granddaughter.

The pattern of our life had been established long ago when Dick and I became best friends in the seventh grade. As husband and wife, we had separate interests, but our daily routine remained the same: conversation, laughter, and closeness.

On a hot August afternoon, Dick looked at me and said, "Pat, the Holy Spirit is dealing with me. I have lung cancer, and I am not going to make it." He had already reached the point of acceptance of death before he sought medical confirmation.

After three nightmarish weeks in the hospital following surgery, Dick returned home to die, six months later, surrounded by his family. During that time, he said good-bye to good friends and prepared his family to handle life without him. His fabulous sense of humor did not desert him as he faced death with class.

After Dick's funeral, family returned to their homes in distant cities. I was upheld by a large group of lifelong friends who allowed me to give way to fatigue after months of 24-hour care. They became my extended family, sustaining me with food, visits, phone calls, and inclusion in social and family gatherings.

INTRODUCTION

Thoughts of widowhood once were reserved almost exclusively for older adulthood. However, when the Twin Towers of the World Trade Center crumbled on September 11, 2001, the structure of thousands of young lives shattered as well. Women of all ages found their everyday existence reduced to rubble, and the world was reminded that widowhood comes also to the young.

Pictures of smoke and flames devouring buildings of seeming strength and impenetrability have been permanently branded in our memory. Nonetheless, the eternal spirit of hope emerges in those left to cope with the mounting tragedies of our world.

Work for the widow begins at ground zero where the debris of devastation and grief is honestly examined, and finally removed. Reconstruction of life starts slowly, building on a foundation of personal beliefs and religious faith.

This book offers first, a rudimentary blueprint for emergency stability in the immediate stages of loss, followed by more detailed plans for moving through the agony of grief and on to a newly designed life in the future. The writers do not stop when grief is tamed, but continue to guide the widow in her discovery of a new ability to love, to experience joy, and to live with contentment.

Hope for a Widow's Shattered World has been written also to help widows find a spiritual center and an emotional stability, energized by imperishable hope, which destroys futility and becomes a lens for viewing all of life. At last, hope, faith, and the widow's long journey establish an "I-Can" mentality for facing the future with its uncharted challenges and opportunities.

Pages of this book are filled with the voices of other widows. Listen to their pain and anguish, their struggles and questions. Hear their laughter mixed with tears. Delight in their courage and vision, as they claim sustaining hope and recreated life.

PART I
FACING WIDOWHOOD

You have suffered a tremendous loss.

You are experiencing pain that is too raw and strange to describe.

You are faced with decisions that seem impossible to make.

You live among family and friends who, at times, seem to be strangers.

You seem to be a stranger to yourself.

You lose things and find it hard to concentrate.

You function at home and on the job with mere automatic responses.

Dreams, plans for the future, are on hold.

Nothing is the same.

Your husband has died.

You are a widow.

WHAT DOES IT MEAN TO BE A WIDOW?

I HAVE NEVER BEEN THERE, DONE THAT.

Just as the relentless waves take bites out of an unprotected shore, widowhood devoured my strength—even my desire to live. Eventually, fear and desolation receded, and I was amazed at my ferocious determination to savor life again!

The shock and numbness of a husband's death quickly give way to pain and searching. No woman can be prepared for widowhood. Even at the end of a lingering illness, death always comes with a jolt and a shudder. Any sense of relief that suffering has ended is, nonetheless, intertwined with the searing pain of separation and the absolute finality of death. Not only has a precious loved-one ceased to exist, but also life, as it has been lived within the circle of family and friends, has ended. Nothing will ever be the same. Widowhood is a journey; it is not an illness from which one must recover. Widowhood is a stage of life, through which the majority of married women must move, as long as the average woman's life span exceeds that of a man.

Different women will have vastly different experiences, but the process of passage, for most widows, is virtually the same. It begins one step at a time, one day at a time. The widow's walk is long and painful, with few shortcuts available, but the outcome is certain: a new life will emerge, often with surprising strengths and unrealized potential. Joy and laughter can return, but first there is work to do.

THE FACE OF WIDOWHOOD

I hid behind a mask of my own making;
I knew I was no longer the person I used to be.

A widow remembers: "I felt no connection with the face staring at me from the makeup mirror. Foundation, blush, eyeliner, lipstick. Practiced motions touched a facade frozen into numbness. My body felt like a drainpipe, emptied of all emotion. I could not fasten my thoughts on his funeral, less than three hours away. I could only concentrate on the immediate moment; choose dress, shoes, bag—not black, but something subdued, something he would approve of. Jewelry—the pin he gave me on our last anniversary—where was it—someone help me—I must find it, a label that we were in each other's possession—something to attach me to him, even now—a symbol of thoughts too fragmented to express out loud.

"In the car—on the way to the church—my family talked about the weather. I wanted to scream, 'How can you even think of sunshine when we are on the way to bury your father?' Instead, I heard my voice ask if anyone had fed the dog.

"A wave of grief surprised me, shook me, like a spasm. We were entering the sanctuary; momentarily, I stopped, knees shaking. A son, on either side, propelled me forward. The organ music swelled, sounding a familiar melody I could not fully recognize. The congregation stood, looking at us as we walked, dreamlike, to the empty pews marked with velvet ropes. I groped for a reason why our entrance was so labored and difficult—why each footstep was like a journey.

"Much later, I would realize that my community of family and friends had been observing me, for the first time, as a widow, a strange identity that I could neither fathom nor begin to claim for myself. Yet in those public moments, a new truth was beginning to take shape: everything familiar was becoming alien; those closest to me were turning into strangers; and the future had ceased to be. Only now and then did the pastor's words of hope and faith break through my cloud of unknowing, like brilliant rays of sunshine briefly defying the power of a gathering storm.

"I knew when it was almost time for the church bell to peal its funeral benediction. The congregation would be released from the flower-scented sanctuary into the freshness of a spring afternoon. They would stand in little groups, waiting, watching for us to follow the polished cherry wood casket topped with yellow roses. Our diminished family would walk, dry-eyed, walled-off from each other in our valiant struggles not to cry—some of us, most likely, would never allow the roughness of feelings to be bathed with healing tears, nor wrestle meaning from grief's strange mixture of anger and adoration.

"Only the other women, whose husbands were dead, could watch the hushed drama of our lives and know that I was taking my first steps on the inevitable widow's walk."

"W" WORD

"I am a widow." The first time I uttered that word, my voice sounded as if it was from another person; my knees shook, and an acid taste lingered in my mouth.

Women admit they are reluctant to say "single again," which does not distinguish loss from divorce from loss by death. Others prefer to be called "survivors." However, true survivorship can only be realized when widowhood has been acknowledged and grief tamed.

The word "widow" has been in the English language since the twelfth century, and shades of meaning include "to be deprived of something greatly valued or needed," and "to separate." In Sanskrit, the word widow means "empty."

The experience of separation is at the heart of what it means to be a widow. When the husband dies, the wife is separated from:

The loved one
Old routines
Former ways of looking at life
Social friends
Real or imagined security
Sexual intimacy
Accustomed physical touch, cuddling
Plans, visions of the future
A companionable listener
Being "first" in someone's life

Widowhood separates members of the family. The father of her children is gone; one half of parenthood is missing. Her family is fragmented. She often feels separated from her perception of the major strengths of her marriage, yet she must pull the pieces together.

Psychologists declare that the death of a husband is the number one stress event in a woman's life. This is true in every culture, and at every age.

WIDOWHOOD IS—

I struggled to understand what was happening to me; conflicting emotions held me captive. I wanted to escape, to run away, but there was no place to hide.

When lacerated by the devastating pain of grief, the overpowering desire is to be anesthetized from realities too new and frightening to be faced. A tremendous escape mechanism takes over thoughts and actions. Yet the hard, cold fact remains: widowhood must be examined and understood, if a woman is to emerge from this experience not battered, but strengthened, for life ahead. Necessary grief work must be completed without becoming mired down at some point of transition.

As a group of widows share their perceptions, a sisterhood emerges, and untouchable pain begins to surface, allowing renewal to begin.

Widowhood is:

> Pain, numbness, denial
> Loneliness, emptiness, sadness
> Anger, guilt, remorse
> Boredom, aimlessness, helplessness
> Paralyzing fatigue
> Change, facing the unknown
> Lost meaning, vitality, emotion
> Yearning, glorification of the past
> Forgetfulness, disconnection with reality
> Loss of time, living in slow motion
> Depression, fear
> Confusion, inability to reason coherently
> Darkness of the soul
> Total absorption with self

Some women may have sustained other losses as painful as the death of a husband, and eventually moved beyond grief. They may try all the coping skills that worked in prior situations; but they still find themselves mired in misery and pain. The enormity of a widow's grief work is deeply felt, but often poorly understood. This lack of understanding, experienced by the widow and often by her support group, can add to her anguish.

As in all experiences of deep loss, the pain is first excruciating and numbing. Cognitive understanding remains for the days ahead, which seem too distant to envision. Many women have explained feeling overcome and paralyzed by thoughts of the smallest daily chore. What they seldom realize is that widowhood immediately precipitates a total identity crisis.

BITS AND PIECES

I felt like a mirror that had been smashed by an angry fist.

Widowhood fragments life into bits and pieces of existence. Bits of past memories and pieces of present reality are patched together in a haphazard collage.

Days unfold without clear purpose or steady flow. No task can consume more than a sliver of time, since concentration is fleeting and energy is grossly depleted. Each task seems disconnected from any other activity of the day. Only the barest necessities call forth limited effort.

Yet there are things that must be done: dishes to be returned, notes to be written, phone calls to be answered. Bits and pieces of couplehood must be touched and gathered up. His clothes may be hidden in a closet until later disposal, yet fragments of his life must be handled almost daily—medicines to be gathered up, his favorite books and magazines to be straightened, his picture to be dusted.

The heartbreak of these necessary duties leads to the unsettling realization that every moment of life now is tinged with grief, which like a dense fog has crept into every crevice of one's surroundings. Grief cannot be either denied or escaped. However, it is in facing grief that the first tiny rays of hope will begin to pierce the grayness of the soul.

WIDOWHOOD—A PARADIGM SHIFT

*I knew that I was different, "changed," perhaps even strange,
but everyone in my life also seemed different! Why? Why?*

Widowhood is hard work. It is not a condition or a state of being to be endured; it is a process that leads through great pain and suffering to a new way of life, complete with the return of joy and happiness. Widowhood is never a choice; it is an inevitability which death thrusts upon a woman.

However, many choices are called for in the days and months that follow. The most fundamental decision is: "Will I simply endure this experience, seeking distractions until time soothes the raw emotions?" or "Will I work at understanding the uniqueness of my grief and the many demands it places upon me as I struggle to become a whole person, able to enjoy and find meaning in life?" For a period of time, a widow often fluctuates between these options.

A widow's grief is unique, because every relationship in her life instantly changes when her husband dies. She has become "uncoupled," and her singleness initiates an identity crisis that touches everyone in her life. The death of parents, a child, or even a dear friend may be devastating, but her identity is not threatened to the degree it is in widowhood.

A widow becomes somewhat of an enigma to those closest to her. For instance, relationship with her children often becomes different; dad is not there to share parental responsibility. Mom no longer has a counter-balance. The whole structure of home life changes. With young children, mother becomes the sole authority figure, and a period of testing and struggle to understand begins.

Grown children may become either protective or distant, unwilling to share their own grief struggles with each other, or with Mom.

Couples who have been close through the years find their friend's singleness awkward, and a period of distancing seems inevitable. Relationship with in-laws may remain close, but the absence of a key family member casts a different feeling on all gatherings.

A widow's deepest pain often centers on a sensation of separation from her familiar self, brought about by her singleness. She not only must deal with grief, which is the normal reaction to all losses, but she also must "re-invent" herself, re-define herself, as a new and different person, living a solo life. The struggle for new self-understanding is a dynamic part of the work that a widow must undertake.

Becoming a widow is a "paradigm shift." It cries out for a realignment of self. Widowhood is a pilgrimage through pain and loneliness that cannot be bypassed or hurried. However, the end result can be the emergence of a new and stronger person.

UNDERSTANDING GRIEF

I thought grief was a lingering sadness, which I could wait out. Instead, it became an all-consuming monster, which lived beyond my grasp.

Grief is the reaction to loss. Loss is an unchangeable, irreversible fact that shatters life into a million pieces. Grief is not the loss, but rather a reaction that encompasses the total person—physically, emotionally, and spiritually. Usually the raw emotions surface first. These strong feelings often are conflicting, swirling, and uncontrollable. There is no escape from grief.

Grief is like a ravenous monster that attempts to gobble up the whole person. However, different people can perceive grief differently. For example, the surge of tears with its intense sorrow may be a lengthy period for some women, while for others it may be quite short.

Grief is most often experienced in recognizable stages and waves. These stages include shock and disbelief, the flood of tears, anger, guilt, acceptance and a return to life. The average widow touches most of these experiences, although in varying order and intensity. Grief is not a linear experience. A widow may repeatedly slip in and out of these stages.

Grief is work; it is necessary. Failure to grieve can result in various health problems and emotional hang-ups. The re-discovery of joy and the return to a full life depend on the willingness to experience the pain of loss and work through a variety of challenges.

Grief work takes time; it cannot be hurried. People who have not experienced the death of a husband may say that a widow should be fine after a year. This is seldom true. The pain diminishes, but sadness lingers. A widow must resist any preconceived timetable.

VOICES OF GRIEF

Grief is like a black hole at the center of life,
with daily living going on around the edges.

"I feel the darkness. Everything inside of me is gray. I feel like I am being swallowed by a thick fog. I can't find my way; I am confused. I have no direction for my life. I am lost, there is no way out; the grayness is too vast. What is happening to me? Am I losing my mind?"

"I feel like I am living on another planet, separated by time and space."

"I don't react in familiar ways. Some days I have an unending flow of tears. Other days I am too frozen inside to cry."

"I don't know where I am in all this. I may still be in shock. On the day of my husband's funeral, I looked in the mirror and thought 'O my God, I don't want to be a widow.'"

"The word 'widow' didn't occur to me until months after my husband died. I was filling out a form at the doctor's office. I left marital status blank. The nurse questioned me. I remember saying 'I am a widow.' The words rang in my ears and tasted peculiar to my lips as I said them. I almost had a physical reaction as I announced, out loud, for the first time, my new identity. I had not 'felt' terribly different until that moment."

"Widowhood is the pits. I lived all my adult life with a mate, then when I got to a point in my life when I really needed help, he died and left me. My health isn't good. I want to be free of responsibilities, and I have to learn a lot of new things—like how to program the VCR."

"I was furious because my husband died so young. When the death certificate came, listing cigarette smoking as the secondary cause of death, I went into a blind rage. Then I felt so guilty about my anger. I buried myself in my work and delayed the period of intense pain and deep sadness. Finally, I went to a counselor to get help in sorting out my emotions."

"Some of my friends mean well, but they say things that upset me for days."

"Loss of a child breaks your heart; loss of a husband breaks your heart and your home."

"I miss men—their conversation, their viewpoints. I miss physical touching, hugs, kisses."

"When my husband died, he took my mind with him, and I wish he would send it back!"

"In grief, you question your own life and its content; you face your own mortality."

"When my husband died, I felt like part of my body was gone. I felt naked, and I was embarrassed to go out in public without him. I was 58, and knew I would feel the same if I lived to be 80. I now have lived longer as a widow than as a married person. After many years, some memories fade, but thoughts of my married life are as much a part of me as my childhood memories."

"Losing a husband is like being stabbed in the heart. The wound heals, but the knife stays."

"Grief is like being in a plastic box. I could see what was going on around me, but I could not participate."

GRIEF'S PRIVATE LANGUAGE

I longed to tell someone what I was feeling, but words were too hollow, too empty to carry the weight of my grief. When I needed most to shout out my pain, I was made mute by the fear of frightening away people who had not encountered earth-shattering, mind-numbing loss.

All experiences are defined by language. We think in words; our dreams and goals are delineated by language. The pain and confusion of grief are intensified because words become inadequate to communicate the depth of this experience. Words become empty and hollow.

There is no recognized vocabulary for grief. In the early stage of loss, shock allows the mind to close down. Logical thought is impossible at times, and random thoughts seem uncontrollable.

Wordlessness can be a mental defense mechanism, stemming from an attempt to shut out and deny anything that brings intense pain. Emotionalism often causes embarrassment. For example, a widow's public tears are likely to be followed by her profuse apologies, and enormous guilt is felt by the person who may have precipitated the emotional release. Instead of accepting this as a normal phase of a painful stage of life, most people are thrown off balance. There are no rehearsals for life or death. At times, one simply must blunder through difficult situations with all of the compassion and honesty that one can muster.

In our culture, death is a taboo subject, stripped from polite conversation. Hence, most people have little experience in framing their thoughts and feelings into words. Perhaps Easter sermons at church form the most prolonged account of death, with the accompanying message of hope beyond the grave. When ultimate realities touch family or friends, unspoken questions and strange feelings defy verbalization. Sharing ceases. Distance grows. Isolation and loneliness deepen.

Family and support-givers of all kinds are touched with the fear of saying something that will seem inappropriate or intensify sadness. Therefore, they retreat into awkward silence. Friends are often afraid of asking bereaved persons how they are, for fear that an honest answer will leave them with no comfortable response.

The bereaved person is extremely fragile and vulnerable. Caregivers must be willing to become vulnerable themselves. Their reluctance to come forward may be resented by the bereaved person. However, at other times their efforts to help may be rebuffed.

After the stylized rituals of casseroles and funeral service, the journey of the bereaved is virtually uncharted. A widow's questions often include "How am I doing? Am I on schedule?" The better question might be, "Will you listen and help me find the words to describe what I am feeling and experiencing right now?"

UNENDING LISTS: A WIDOW'S SELF-PORTRAIT

I cried with understanding at the honest confession of a newfound sister-in-suffering. Her ways of coping became a thread of hope for me.

"As a widow, I lived by lists. Without them I could not have gotten through the endless days and the interminable nights since my husband's death. On a good day, I could mark off two or three of the twenty some-odd items I had scrawled on a yellow legal pad.

"Mostly, I stayed in the house behind closed doors and shuttered windows. I allowed the answering machine to take most phone calls. Trying to carry on any kind of conversation was simply too exhausting. Close friends thought after two months I was ready to be "distracted" into a more cheery mood. There was no way to tell them what I was feeling; they were not tough enough to really want to know. I was the first widow in our circle of friends, and they did not know what to say or do.

"I ventured into the world of supermarkets, pharmacies, and banks only when dire needs arose. With shopping finished, I would drive aimlessly through my neighborhood, up and down streets, drained of their familiarity by a feeling of disconnection with life. I would do anything to postpone returning to the emptiness of the house I once called home. Occasionally, I would make a wrong turn, and momentarily panic in my lostness.

"At times I was terrified of losing my mind. I could not recall my next door neighbor's name for a whole morning. I was constantly losing keys and pens, bills and reading glasses. I felt as if I was out of control, being sucked into a vacuum of murky darkness from which there was no escape."

EMOTION-CHARGED EXISTENCE

Other losses in my life had been equally painful,
but none had made me question my own identity.

No matter how a woman reacts to the death of her husband, at some point she probably will wonder if her behavior is "normal." She may become frightened if she cries constantly and uncontrollably, while another woman may worry because she is hardly able to cry at all.

Two such women share their very different reactions to their loss:

"For a long time, my life seemed strewn with sharp-edged feelings. Tears remained near the surface, ready to overflow at unexpected moments. Waves of memories would return, unbidden, washing me in unutterable sadness. Moments later, thoughts of shared joy would bring laughter and healing sweetness. Only physical exhaustion seemed to slow the roller coaster ride of these wild feelings."

Another widow explains:

"My experience was quite different. I desperately wanted to cry, hoping a flood of tears would break the dam of suppressed pain and loss that remained deep inside, untouched and inarticulate. My dry and brittle spirit robbed me of much needed companionship. Princess Diana died two years after my husband's death, but as I watched her funeral on TV, I began to sob, and I cried all weekend. I felt so weird!"

There is no "correct" way to deal with the gamut of emotions that assault a widow. Unrelated triggers can release surprising outbursts of suppressed feelings. However, the response of each woman will be somewhat conditioned by her age, personality, life experience, and the very culture into which she was born.

JOUSTING WITH DRAGONS

Dragon attacks occur early in widowhood when women are too exhausted and preoccupied with survival to recognize their presence. Dragons are all-consuming emotions, feelings that control and overpower the person.

Long forgotten scars from old resentments and disappointments may begin to surface and can become gigantic in the aftermath of loss. They often set up barriers to facing grief. Unfinished business must be dealt with.

Weighed down by grief, a widow's first tendency is to deny any additional stress which drains away limited energy. However, facing painful emotions can mark the emergence from earlier frozen feelings of shock and numbness.

There is real danger in avoiding negative, hopeless feelings. Any distraction or excuse can be used to postpone this hard work. Many people stuff down their feelings, saying they do not have the strength to do this part of grief work. The truth is that energy can be found when we wrestle with dragons on the prowl.

Three of the most dangerous dragons are fear, anger, and loneliness.

Fear may begin to take shape before death occurs. One widow explains, "At the first diagnosis of my husband's cancer, I felt as if everything inside me turned to ice, as if ice water were coursing through my veins. My body reacted to this coming horror, but my mind could not grasp the fear that threatened to consume me."

Fear which inflicts deep wounds includes:
Fear of being alone
Fear of not being able to cope with illness and death
Fear of not having enough money
Fear of losing the home
Fear of mounting medical bills
Fear of maintaining one's life style
Fear of the future
Fear of handling the spouse's responsibilities
Fear of full parental responsibilities

Fear of making mistakes
Fear of the unknown

Anger is almost a universal component of grief. Anger can cover a range of emotion from mere annoyance to rage. Anger has a wide spectrum including:

Anger at the deceased spouse
Anger at the doctors
Anger at the family
Anger at well-meaning friends
Anger at oneself
Anger at God

Some women may experience only brief spurts of irritation. For others, anger may linger for months or years. Anger can be translated into antagonism or resentment over inconsequential or unrelated things. Anger engenders a feeling of victimization.

Loneliness can be the most long-lived dragon. Even after a degree of happiness and contentment has returned, floating episodes of isolation can cause unexpected sadness and yearning for the past.

Loneliness spawns feelings of hopelessness.
Loneliness warps reality and can lead to depression.
Loneliness deafens one to words of encouragement offered by others.
Loneliness wounds; solitude heals.

Solitude is the loneliness dragon slain.
Solitude is the ability to be alone without being lonely.
Solitude provides a quiet, calming space.

When dragons are faced, dissected, and their many parts labeled, a plan of action can be designed to slay the beasts.

TAMING THE DRAGONS

Each person has a private set of emotions to subdue. Dragons may hover around constantly or vanish completely for a while, only to reappear later in unpredictable locations. Such mood altering, gut grabbing feelings and thoughts may be found:

<u>In specific places</u>
Home
Church
Parties, especially dinner parties
Favorite restaurants
Family gatherings

<u>At certain times</u>
Holidays
Weekends
Anniversaries
Mornings or evenings

The onset of some emotions is predictable. Other feelings seem to spring up unbidden.

<u>Obvious Dragons</u>
Strategies can be planned in advance of a full-blown attack.
Dragons met head-on are easier to tame.

<u>Hidden Dragons</u>
Surprise attacks inflict deep wounds.
Preparation time is limited for taming or destroying them.
Floating fear results.

No matter the origin, overpowering emotions can be conquered.

<u>Assault strategies</u>
When you need specific help, ask for it.
Gain strength and insight from friends, family, counselors, pastors etc.
Try to maintain a calm center.
Work from a mental plan.
Sustain realistic expectations.
Persevere, persevere, persevere.
Don't obsess about failures.
Build up your self-confidence.
Have faith in God.

LOSSES

I told a new acquaintance that I had lost my husband,
but in truth I was the one who was lost.

All losses produce pain and discomfort; a grieving process is lived through, whether or not it is recognized as grief. Children are initiated into this universal experience when a pet dies, when a special plant is killed by frost, or when a family member dies—often a grandparent or distant relative.

Dealing with a loss can be similar to solving a follow-the-numbers puzzle. Only when all the dots are connected does a picture emerges. All of our losses are connected. Each new cause for grief brings with it some of the remembered pain or unfinished business from past losses. If grief in the past has been experienced and dealt with positively, a sense of hope and self-confidence is evident, even in widowhood.

By the time many women have become widows, they have already lived through a variety of such losses. They may have buried one or both parents, significant friends, or perhaps a child. Even the youngest widows have lived through a variety of broken relationships and lost dreams. Since grief of any kind follows a similar pattern, a widow may not realize that her new grief includes facets unduplicated by the other losses she has endured. Recognition of the uniqueness of a widow's experience will provide concrete focus for much of the necessary grief work that lies ahead.

For example, a woman may try all the coping skills that worked in a prior loss, but still find herself mired in misery and pain. A widow's grief work often is deeply felt, but poorly understood by both herself and those around her, thus intensifying her anguish.

LIFE AT A CRAWL

The energy of love had drained away.
Each day was a long journey tread in slow motion.

"Love is the dipstick of our pain. The degree to which we have loved is the measure of our loss. If you love deeply, you have to be willing to be hurt deeply, but that's a hell of a lot better than the other alternative—not loving at all," according to a woman whose husband died after a brief, but traumatic, illness.

A widow's capacity to love others is temporarily diminished after her spouse's death. She often is totally self-absorbed and afraid to engage her deepest self, yet she desperately yearns for the love that is now lost, and wants someone to provide it for her. She wants love as a passive experience. She is incapable, in the early stages of grief, to give deeply to a new person in her life. She is looking for a care-taker. Quick re-marriages often fail.

When a widow reaches the point of reciprocal love, she has, to some degree, become a changed person. Only then can she know and understand the man to whom she would be willing to give her deepest self.

A widow has returned to wholeness when she can actively love. Love is not an option in life; it is a necessity! "Love or perish."

Widows need little love exercises on the way to wholeness: love of children, friends, pets, nature, anything that moves her to actively care for needs beyond herself.

Slowly, a widow must understand and love the new self whom she is becoming. Then, with growing desire, discipline, and determination, she can accept widowhood and move beyond it.

MATTERS THAT CAN'T WAIT[1]

I thought I was getting back to normal when I could find momentary pleasure in a
wild shopping spree. However, when I finally totaled the bills,
I was shocked to discover that I was flirting with financial disaster.

The last thing most widows want to face and deal with is money matters. However, financial concerns may be among the first things she must tackle. Her mind may not be ready to compute numbers, nor is she always prepared to make wise and careful decisions, calculating their impact on her future.

If her husband managed business matters, she may feel overwhelmed and paralyzed. Many older women confess they have never had to pay monthly bills or reconcile their checkbooks. Younger working women may have more financial savvy, but their income may be more drastically diminished. In either case, monthly bills cannot be neglected.

As soon as possible, a widow needs to get an over-all picture of her financial status. Frugality and caution during the first year will prevent costly mistakes. Big-ticket items should be avoided, if possible. Hidden costs loom ahead: taxes on inheritance, income, and property, and lawyer's fees, as well as the more obvious cost of insurance on cars, home, and health.

Advice from family and friends should be considered carefully. Consultation with a trusted professional can be helpful, but the widow must make all decisions herself. She will make mistakes along the way, but hopefully not disastrous ones.

The first impulse to sell the home should be resisted for at least a year, unless the cash is needed to survive. Many widows with a secure financial future may feel penniless and panicked at first, but with time they can develop a more realistic assessment of their situation.

---

1. See Addendum, Peace of Mind—Financial Management for Life

FIRST AID FOR DAILY LIVING

New widows should not be allowed to handle sharp knives. I sliced open my finger instead of slicing the bread. As I fumbled through the first aid box, I longed for a Band-Aid for my lacerated feelings.

Excessive sleeping

Reluctance to get out of bed can become an escape technique. A conscious decision must be made to get up, get dressed, and perform at least one function a day. As one widow stated, "You have to keep putting one foot in front of the other, knowing that one day it will be better."

Eating

Eating alone can be a painful experience. Many widows say they cannot sit at the same table that they shared with their husbands. "I will never forget standing at the kitchen sink, eating out of a peanut butter jar," confessed a widow of 15 years. Some find it helpful to eat in a different room, while watching TV or reading a book.

When children are involved, the dinner table can become a place for them to act out their unexpressed grief. Return to a normal schedule as soon as possible, and help children verbalize their feelings. Let mealtime be an opportunity to remember Dad with humor and fondness.

Many widows eat either too much or too little. When battling stress, food can be used as a distraction during long, empty hours. Unfortunately, to the detriment of their body, certain unhealthy meals can be mistakenly relished as sources of comfort. A healthy diet and exercising can help overcome normal depression.

To other women, the very thought of food may be nauseous. Any effort to cook may require more concentration than is available in the early stages of widowhood. If she lives alone, cooking for one may be a new experience which she is not ready to tackle. Even grocery shopping may call for decisions that are trouble-some. A variety of frozen foods can provide a helpful alternative. Junk food should be avoided.

Eating out can be helpful. One widow made the conscious decision to leave the house once a day, often for lunch.

Undefined pain[1]

Widowhood engenders a variety of health concerns. Stress and grief can mask very real problems. All physiological systems have been impacted by loss. The immune system has been grossly compromised. Free-floating aches and pains are typical, but should not be ignored if persistent. A doctor's examination can help sort out a variety of complaints. Minor disturbances are characteristic, and some-times disappear when in the company of understanding family or friends.

Emotional pain also can be free-floating and seem to be of indiscernible ori-gin. "I was completely devastated, but I knew I had to get to the bottom of my pain," stated a woman who had been married nearly fifty years. "I finally realized that the point of greatest fulfillment in my marriage was now the cause of my deepest ache. I could give him up as a husband, but not as a friend."

When she identified the intimacy of friendship as the source of greatest fulfill-ment in her marriage, she also discovered the point of her deepest loss. In so doing, she became more open to true friendship with other widows and with a close circle of people who cared deeply about her. From them, she gradually began to draw strength and find moments of pleasure.

Irrational fears

Widowhood is full of emotions that seem very strange. Many women admit ques-tioning their own sanity when having trouble concentrating, making decisions, expressing themselves, remembering appointments, or recalling names.

"What terrified me more than anything else was my loss of time," confessed a recent widow. "I would sit on the edge of the bed, staring into space, never know-ing if I sat there a few minutes or an hour. Often I only looked at the front page of the newspaper to see what day it was."

---

1.   See Addendum, Take Care of Yourself—Twenty Things You Should Know About Staying Healthy

Another widow was terrified by what she called "things that go bump in the night." This included the creaking and groaning of the house, a leaky toilet which flushed itself at 1 a.m., weird animal sounds, sighing of the wind and the crash of thunder.

"It helps to look for logical explanations for our fears," laughed a third widow who had been greatly disturbed when her doorbell rang at 1 a.m. The next day it rang at 5 a.m. Each time she looked out, but no one was in sight. Finally, her neighbor across the street solved the mystery. He saw a bird pecking away at her doorbell.

Sharing fears with other widows and reading about widowhood help a woman discover that many of her questionable experiences are quite common, and diminish with understanding.

Family Friction

It is easy for a widow to be so consumed with her own grief that the feelings of other family members are ignored. She may conclude that her family is cold and uncaring if they do not readily sense her deep needs and respond in ways she desires. Yet, they also are wrestling with their own emotions, which may not be as life-changing as hers, but can be equally painful. Each family member may be hiding behind the intention not to "upset" the other, or afraid of losing control of his or her own feelings.

Many widows may be operating on the very raw edge of existence. Often a small, insignificant happening can erupt in a tirade of hurtful words not related to the instance at hand.

In the days immediately following death, non-verbal communication is the most effective. Hugs and handholding are powerful, because the pain is too deep for words to touch. As feelings begin to be articulated, large doses of forbearance and forgiveness may be called for. As time passes, sharing tears, doubts, and anxiety helps others more quickly assess the widow's needs.

Small children often act out their unique dismay and baffling fears. Their basic fear of abandonment must be quickly and reassuringly met by Mom, who may be able to give very little warmth. Friends and other family members can step in with back-up support.

The degree of closeness or separation within a family is in proportion to the openness of gut-level confession and expression.

IMPOSSIBILITY

I had been a self-confident and successful business woman. Now I felt successful if I made a peanut butter sandwich and a cup off coffee at the same time.

"Impossibility" may be the word that often describes a widow's life during the first days and weeks immediately following her husband's funeral. Her conversation may be full of incomplete sentences, reflecting only fragmentary thoughts. Simple tasks may be interrupted by the search for misplaced items or forgotten commitments and appointments.

One widow said she was horrified to find herself attempting to put her clothes in the freezer instead of the washing machine. This can be a frightening time for a woman; she may question her sanity, adding another fear to a growing list of anxieties, many of which she may not want to admit to herself, must less to other people.

There are times when she desperately needs companionship, and there are times when she seeks solitude in order to be alone with her tears and unpredictable emotions.

During these anxious days, she needs a person with whom she can share her conflicting thoughts and inexplicable behavior. However, she must be careful in choosing such a confidant. Only another widow can truly understand the depth of her state of being. Many women confess that their own widowed mother gave the most beneficial support and guidance.

Widows need to avoid controlling people with their list of "should's" and "should not's." Each woman experiences the stages of widowhood in her own individual way. Professional counselors and clergy are helpful, but studies reveal only a small percentage of widows are in need of clinical help.

FRIENDS

Compassionate, caring friends have loved life back into me,
while the cold forgetfulness of others stabbed my already aching heart.

"Friends really surprised me," declared a young widow. "Several were not the same after my husband's death. Some, whom I thought would be supportive, actually disappeared. Others, whom I had not expected to be supportive, amazed me with their attention. Simple thoughtfulness translated into a major blessing: a card, phone call, or bowl of soup brightened gray days of the soul."

Some married women reluctantly confess that they don't want a widow around their husbands. A husband's best friend also may end the relationship with the widow because the center of that friendship was between the men; the wife was merely an appendage. When the husband is gone, such a friend may rarely give the widow another thought.

Nonetheless, friendships are important. Some of the best support comes from friends because they are not as intimately involved in many critical issues as are family members. Friends who disappoint should not be judged too harshly. They cannot truly understand, unless they have lost a spouse.

As a single person, the widow may seek new friends among women who have similar interests. Care should be taken in selecting new male friends. Rushing into a serious relationship too soon may be disastrous. Unfortunately, it is easy for someone to take advantage of a widow struggling with grief. In the early stages of widowhood, it is impossible for a woman to know what kind of a person she may ultimately become, nor will she know the type of companionship she might want at a later time.

Friends can be helpful in many ways:

> Bring food
> Call on the phone
> Share their family events
> Listen without judgment
> Give advice sparingly

Share tears and laughter
Share memories
Never put a time-limit on grief

Platitudes friends should avoid:

"I know how you feel." (unless they are also widows)
"It was God's will: God needed him."
"He just went to sleep." (Never say this to a child.)
"You should be O.K. now that it's been six months."
"All you need is a distraction."
"Time heals everything."

FINDING A COMFORT ZONE

My life had become a patchwork of both pain and comfort. Simple acts of kindness and old routines provided momentary stability and peace.

A group of widows shared what had brought them the most comfort:

People who phone, bringing unexpected moments of kindness
Cards, which communicate "you are not forgotten"
Acceptance, no matter how bleak one's mood might be
Shared experiences with other widows
Competent advisors (financial, pastoral)
Shared memories with friends
Family togetherness
Help with carpooling to children's activities
Social activities with friends of long standing
Work
Movies, two hours of escape from misery and pain
Peace from nature
Journal of one's thoughts
Books on widowhood
Religious faith
Church fellowship
Worship
Prayer and meditation
Realization that no matter how many people or distractions are in a widow's life, grief is essentially <u>a do-it-yourself activity</u>.

FAITH IN FACING WIDOWHOOD

*For the first time in my life, I flung sharp-edged questions at God; then I turned my
back, like a pouting child waiting for answers to my unanswerable queries.*

Widowhood is a cracking open of one's being; it is a desperate, if unconscious,
search for meaning in the face of death. Sometimes there is anger at the spouse,
and often anger, reluctantly admitted, toward God. Questions may swirl in the
widow's mind as she asks, "Why, God?"

"Why? Why did this happen?"

"Why did God allow this to happen to me?"

"Did God take my husband?"

All of her questions must be faced and dealt with. The widow does not need to
be condemned for her doubts or to be preached to by well-meaning friends. She
needs to find a theology of grief that is not simplistic, but yet simple to understand. In a time of spiritual turmoil, when doubts may be more prevalent than
convictions, the widow needs one or two basic truths to hang onto until her mind
begins to clear and her heart begins to heal.

In the early days of grief, fundamental beliefs emerge:

1.God did not cause my husband's death.

2.God stands with me to take me through my loss and pain.

Greater Biblical understanding and theological reasoning can come later.

When grief is new and raw, it may be helpful to have a few verses of Scripture
to cling to:

"The Lord is near to the brokenhearted." Psalm 34:18

*"In my distress I called upon the Lord; to my God I cried for help. From his temple he
heard my voice, and my cry to him reached his ears.* Psalm 18:6

Jesus said, "I will never leave you, nor forsake you." Hebrews 13:5

Women who have lived a life of strong religious faith may ask different questions. Their wondering can be within a well-defined structure of beliefs and often centers more on specific details of life after death. They may ask such questions as:

> "Where is heaven; what is it like?"
> "What does one do in heaven?"
> "Will I see my husband again; will he know me?"

These questions may be baffling and unanswerable, but they usually are asked with more hope than doubt. These widows believe in life after death and the unfathomable reality of heaven. Yet faith in God and a firm belief in life eternal do not provide immunity from the emotions of grief. Faith does not mean bypassing uncertainty, fear, or risk. Instead, faith offers a guiding hand and the warmth and encouragement of hope for a hard and sometimes frightening journey.

VOICES OF THE FAITHFUL

Looking back, I believe God was the closest to me when God seemed absent.
The mystery of faith never ceases to amaze me!

A widow remembers:

"Our family life revolves around church activities; one of us is there nearly every day. This didn't change when Ben was diagnosed with leukemia. I continued to chair the missions committee, oversaw the preparation of Thanksgiving dinner for the homeless, substituted as a Sunday School teacher; yet I felt detached from everyone around me. I said the right faith words, all the while, wondering where God was in my unraveling life.

"Looking back, I realize that 'going to church' has been almost a life-long habit in my life—a powerful routine that formed a structure of stability in those torturous days of denial and pain.

"I admit that often the Sunday sermon sailed past me, with only a snippet of thought staying with me, but that fragment of faith was often my lifeline for the week. Surprisingly, my greatest help came from the words of old hymns of my childhood. 'Blessed Assurance' rang in my ears for weeks, as did 'Leaning on the Everlasting Arms.' I don't remember much that was said at Ben's funeral, but I recall following the casket from the church while the congregation sang 'How Firm a Foundation.'

"It was hard to go back to church the next Sunday after Ben was gone. I avoided the pew where we had sat for years. Instead, I tried to hide on the back row. Nonetheless I was there, and that blessed routine kept me among a family of faith which loved me into an awareness of God's power holding me up, even when thoughts and feelings were paralyzed."

Another widow explains:

"I am a clergy woman who has conducted countless funerals through the years. I have an extensive language of faith and hope to help navigate through the shadow of death. Yet when confronted by the terminal illness of my husband, those very words became porous, all their meaning leaking away. I understood the theology of life and death, but I knew little of the intense agony of losing a spouse.

"We had spent the entire afternoon in the hospital emergency room, trying to determine the cause of his sudden, unbearable, pain. Finally the unexpected diagnosis came: cancer. Three months.

"The approach of death rendered me senseless, and I was not the patient. Gently, our doctor gave me a simple task to move me through the awfulness of the moment. I was to go to the admitting desk, while he minimally explained the hospital stay to my husband.

"With the paper work completed, I embarked on what seemed like an unthinkable journey to his tenth-floor room. As I stepped from the elevator, I was confronted by a wall of glass overlooking the sprawling downtown skyline. The familiar, graceful architecture of towering buildings was silhouetted against the most intense, flaming red sunset I had ever seen. I stopped, mesmerized by the beauty laid out before me.

I stood, immobilized by shock and exhaustion, amazed that a whole day had slipped away. Suddenly, powerfully, a wordless truth swept over me with a certainty beyond any possible doubt: God was in the sunset, and also there in the hospital corridor, and God would get us through whatever lay ahead.

"The wordless promise embedded in that scene was fulfilled in the following five months of intense suffering and extreme tension. Often my prayers were more deep, soul-felt yearnings, than carefully articulated words. My faith, theological understanding, and faith practices, formed the crucible into which the reality of death could be endured and mourned, and the oasis for the return of joy and the goodness of life."

VOICES OF SCRIPTURE

I could not sit still to read the Bible, and only fragments of Scripture would come to mind. A friend gave me a card with verses from the Psalms. I kept it in my pocket and read it a dozen times throughout the day

I am weary with my moaning; every night I flood my bed with tears. I drench my couch with my weeping. My eyes waste away because of grief.
Psalm 6:6-7

My God, my God, why have you forsaken me?
Why are you so far from helping me, from the words of my groaning?
O my God, I cry by day, but you do not answer,
and by night, but find no rest. Psalm 22:1-2

Be gracious to me, O Lord, for I am in distress;
my eye wastes away from grief,
my soul and body also.
For my life is spent with sorrow, and my years with sighing;
my strength fails because of my misery,
and my bones waste away...
But I trust in you, O Lord;
I say, "You are my God."
My times are in your hand...
Let your face shine upon your servant; save me in your steadfast love...
Be strong, and let your heart take courage,
all you who wait for the Lord. Psalm 31:9-10, 14, 15a, 16, 24

Give ear to my prayer, O God;
do not hide yourself from my supplication.
Attend to me, and answer me;
I am troubled in my complaint.
Psalm 55:1-2

Do not fear, for I am with you,
do not be afraid, for I am your God;
I will strengthen you, I will help you,
I will uphold you with my victorious right hand. Isaiah 41:10

Blessed are those who mourn, for they will be comforted
Matthew 5:4

A WIDOW'S PRAYER

I cannot be formal, and compose a lovely prayer,. but, O God, I need to talk to you.

Lord God, I need desperately to know you are with me, even though I don't feel your presence. I call your name, and sit in silence, because I have no words of my own. O, God—Creator—Father—my Father...*Our Father who is in heaven*...is my husband in heaven with You?

I offer the only words I can remember: *hallowed be Your name*...holy, special God, your Son knew death...You are a suffering God...You know my pain...

Your kingdom come:....Gather me into your peace, your justice, your healing...

Your will be done on earth as it is in heaven:...You did not will my husband's death...You have received him unto Yourself...Do you cry with me...?

Give us this day our daily bread...I am starving for strength, energy to live again...sustain me, one day at a time...

Forgive us as we forgive others...Forgive me for my anger at him for dying—my anger at You...

Lead us not into temptation, but deliver us from evil...I feel as if all my defenses are gone...I don't know how to go on...Please just hold me in the hollow of your hand...

Yours is the kingdom, and power, and glory forever...I think I believe that...Yes, I do...O God, help me...

PART II
WORKING THROUGH GRIEF

WIDOW'S WORK

"How long does it take for grief to go away?" I asked another widow. She asked me,
"What have <u>you</u> done to help make grief go away?"

Grief work must begin in the mind. Everything that is done to work through grief externally is first a conscious thought. Working through grief is an intentional decision. Nothing is going to happen externally until it happens internally; therefore, thoughts are highly significant, and can be controlled. The mental processing of deep feelings can change morbidity to hopefulness.

Grief work begins with the recognition that the widow is a "different" person. This includes a willingness to face the pain; look it in the eye, saying, "I am not O.K. I will be, but I am not yet O.K. I am not the person I used to be, but I am still a person. I will not always be the person I am today. I will become someone whom I can not yet identify."

This is not an easy task. It takes work to overcome grief and become whole again. It will not occur automatically. There are many reasons why people may not choose to do their grief work. Everyday decisions can be so demanding that feelings are put aside, causing individuals to lose touch with themselves and become unaware of their real, underlying emotions.

Widowhood encompasses multiple losses, such as the loss of friends, social life, and financial security, in addition to the loss of her husband. This can seem too overwhelming to be dealt with.

The fear of change also is one of the major reasons grief work is shunned. Change is painful, and the thought of enduring added stress can have a paralyzing effect. With physical energy at low ebb, familiar discomfort can be easier and more appealing than the unknown.

If a woman is the first in her family or circle of friends to become a widow, she may not have the guidance and understanding for the work to be done. Many women declare that other widows gave them their most meaningful help by becoming role models. Without someone to talk openly to, feelings, questions, fears, may remain locked inside, causing the person to become "stuck" in her grief.

A woman may attempt to follow an already established pattern of dealing with pain and loss, but that old pattern may fail her now. Former methods must be examined and rejected or modified to find a new pattern that will work. For example, a person may have reacted to another earlier loss with anger and its accompanying adrenaline rush to see her through a difficult time. But in widowhood, deep sadness laced with fear may be a new and baffling experience.

Grief work is like peeling an onion; a person may cry through many layers of losses to get to the one emotion which must be dealt with, which frees her to become whole again, and fully functional.

QUESTIONS TO PONDER

My very being seemed twisted and bent into a question mark. All certainty in my life had been washed away by my never-ending tears.

How do you face grief?

> Identify areas of greatest pain; call the pain by name.
> Break problems into small pieces; take one small step at a time.

How do you endure grief?

> Accept the new reality, knowing that one day the pain will lessen.

How do you overcome grief?

> Find meaning in the midst of loss.

How long does it take to grieve?

> There is no time limit; things are better after a year.

How do you move beyond grief?

> Realize that a widow's life has been shattered, but she can be whole again. Plans can be made with joyful expectations, even if elements of residual pain are sometimes triggered by unexpected, illogical things.

How does the length of marriage affect grief?

> Usually, the longer two people share their intimate selves, the greater the pain of grief. A more lengthy history of togetherness leaves a long legacy of habits and memories, which can both bless and burn. However, it is not the duration of marriage, but rather the degree of intimacy that is the barometer of pain.

How crucial is the personality of the woman?

A widow's self-understanding and life style are important. If she had been an independent person in the family, most likely she will deal better with widowhood than if she were a shy, dependant person whose whole focus had been centered on her husband and family.

UNDOING THE MARRIAGE MYTH

The terror of my aloneness rose up to strangle me whenever I had to make major decisions without his counsel or concern: when I had to replace a leaky roof, when I had to have the car repaired, when I had to go to bed with the flu.

Widows face the undoing of the "marriage myth." Even modern, liberated women harbor faint longings for a man who will guard her, keep her safe, fulfill her, and be a pleasant companion, even if great happiness and congeniality are not part of the bargain. This idealized, acculturated longing may be unconscious, but the unmasking in widowhood can cause such romantic notions to surface. Older women may accept these expectations as the norm, while younger women may be shocked to find they ever entertained such desires.

Hope springs eternal, even in an unhappy marriage. There is usually the dream that things might get better. The familiarity of a bad situation is often preferred over the frightening possibilities of change. The unknown looms larger than the pain. Sometimes, in a miserable marriage, or after a prolonged and painful illness, death comes as a release, and often a sense of guilt may follow.

Even if her husband was less than loving, less than ideal by anyone's standards, some widows may glorify the deceased and remember him far bigger than life. Another woman may go through the process of recalling only the negative traits, and diminish the real person; or she may make him the object of her hatred, and remember him as even worse than he was!

Memories are extremely subjective and easily distorted. These extremes in thinking are normal and subject to emotional mood swings. The unrelenting task of the widow is to come to a realistic assessment of her spouse. This takes much time and is a product of the widow's own personal growth.

At the time of death, and following the funeral, a woman may be assaulted by different images of her husband from those shared by friends and relatives. A workaholic may be idolized by his company, but resented by his wife. The view presented by in-laws, the community, or the church may present differing descriptions of the same person.

Hopefully, with time, the widow will be able to savor the sweetness of her marriage without shunning the disappointments and failures which are part of life. A realistic assessment of the past leads to healthy expectations of the future.

A widow explained: "I was paralyzed by thoughts of trying to manage life without David. I moaned about how he did everything for me! Then, I began to remember how his law practice consumed so much of this time and energy. I recalled how capably I had handled several family crises when he was not there. Little by little, I realized I probably could face the future—alone."

TRUTH CONFESSED

I soon realized that every widow walks a different path, but everyone must eventually face with brutal honesty whatever lies buried in the past.

A widow shares her deepest secret:

"I knew I could not tell another human being the truth. I was glad that my husband was dead! There, I admit it. At least in my mind, I acknowledged the terrible, tainted fact that frightened me late at night when raw reality could not be denied.

"At first, I wished that I had a priest or pastor to confess my way out of some state of imagined damnation, which must be somewhere reserved for such malignant pleasure.

"John's business associates and our friends lauded me for being so stoic and dry-eyed. Lack of emotion is socially accepted for the deathbed and the first days beyond. Our grown children moved quickly back into their own worlds, relieved that mother seemed quite capable of handling the future, whatever that meant.

"I soon savored my new-found independence and freedom to 'march to my own drummer'. Didn't I have a right to feel that way? I argued with myself. I suspected John was having an affair. I never had proof, but I didn't really want to know. By then, we had grown distant and short with one another. However, divorce was never even mentioned. We both had too much to lose. His reputation as a small town doctor was important to him, and the material abundance could buy me luxury, if not happiness. So, 'look the other way and don't rock the boat,' had become my motto. Now the boat was all mine and I could flourish.

"My closest friends told me how good I looked, how happy I seemed, how proud of me they were for handling my situation so well. In the first 18 months, I had worked on my weight and my wardrobe, joined my sister in New York to see the new plays, and gone on a whirlwind tour of the capitals of Europe.

"Now to my befuddlement, floating uneasiness robbed me of delight in freedom to be myself. Outbursts of both tears and temper amazed me and shocked unsuspecting companions. Imagined slights and indignities constantly unnerved me.

"With several of my friends seeing therapists for a variety of reasons, I felt it safe to do the same. In therapy, fierce arguments ensued as I attempted to defend myself against professional wisdom. During one stormy session, my psychologist told me that I was stuck in grief—immobile and deadened. I flared back that I was still in celebration, not grief! Defiantly, I laid out my justification.

"His answering words chilled me with their truth; he demanded that I <u>begin</u> my grief work. 'Each loss in life MUST be grieved,' he explained. 'Your grief work began long before the death of your husband. It started with the loss of your dreams and expectation for your marriage. The death of your family unity occurred long before John's illness began. Unfinished business must be mourned, even if the deceased person is not. Unfinished business can become like a virus to terminally infect those left living'."

JOB DESCRIPTION

Still mired in the ever-present muck of grief, a new possibility took shape; maybe I had to become an active participant to break free of sadness and loneliness. But how? I longed for a blueprint for my life.

Widow's work can be divided into three tasks: surviving, stretching, and moving. These actions also can indicate the stages of widowhood, which are necessary for women to explore.

Surviving requires women to stand on their own two feet, saying, "I will endure." This includes dealing with family, as well as learning how to adequately handle the myriad of everyday responsibilities: grocery shopping, carpooling, balancing the check book, having the car serviced, dealing with repair persons, and doctors.

Stretching begins with a few tentative steps toward more difficult activities, declaring, "I will struggle." This may mean devising a new daily routine, eating alone in a restaurant, driving out of town, going to movies alone, or preparing income tax returns.

Moving is a time of taking action, living out the resolve, "I will grow and change," rather than simply desiring things to be different. This entails doing many new things, experimenting with activities beyond the sphere of one's former life, such as buying a car, redecorating the house, planning a trip to a distant location, working toward abandoned personal goals.

"I WILL ENDURE": SURVIVING

I could not deny the reality of days in which
I was capable of nothing more than breathing.

Immediately following the death of one's husband, survival is the first task at hand for the widow. Often it may be the only task of which the widow is capable. Survival is getting through those first days any way possible. Many women have trouble functioning at all. Some can barely take care of personal hygiene, or even eat food brought in by friends. Often exhaustion comes as a surprise. Concentration is nil. Thoughts are unfocused and fleeting. Some women spend days sitting in a chair or lying on a bed, staring at the ceiling.

"I never knew what time it was, and I had to look at the newspaper to be sure of the day of the week," stated a young widow. "I had canceled all my volunteer work and social obligations. There was no forced structure to my life. I was totally adrift, without focus or immediate responsibilities. One dismal day simply slipped into another."

The presence of children or the demands of a job immediately propel other women back into their daily routine. Family and employers need to know that going through familiar motions does not signify a return to any kind of normalcy. It is possible to operate on "auto-pilot" for a short period of time. However, the need for these women to find new coping skills is crucial.

Every person must get through this period in a very personal way, without listening to a litany of "should's" delivered by friends or family. This is a time for widows to move at their own pace whenever possible.

It is often hard, or impossible, to think beyond the immediate time. Hope—"light at the end of the tunnel"—seems only an illusion. Fear for the future blocks and distorts any movement beyond the barest necessities. A sense of isolation mingles with a pervading sense of neediness. Yet what is needed cannot be clearly envisioned or articulated. Well-meaning family and friends fumble for words and search vainly for something to do to help.

Survival can be a period of intense self-absorption or a time of self-abandon-ment, laced with distractions. Some widows can think of nothing but their pain and loss, while others anesthetize their feelings with constant work or diversions of any kind. A middle course is the most helpful.

The death of a spouse is life's greatest stressor, depleting the immune system and befuddling the brain. Physical illness is more likely during the first two years after such a death. Therefore, timely physical examinations and a healthy life style are necessary. Alcohol and prescription drugs create only an illusion of help, but can have dire or even deadly consequences.

Personal safety is compromised by mental confusion. Driving a car or operat-ing any kind of equipment could be hazardous during the early days of grief. Even cooking can be dangerous. Many women have confessed forgetting food heating on the stove until burning the pan and its contents.

"My daughter thought my former love of shopping had returned when she found a new set of pots and pans in the cupboard. I never told her that I had burned and blackened two pots and a skillet beyond my efforts to clean them up," laughed a former gourmet cook. Some women have declared microwave cooking the safest method until thought processes return to normal. Eating out can provide another alternative, with the added benefit of being around other people, thus breaking the solitary syndrome.

SEPARATE WORK ORDERS

I timidly attended a recovery group. The women talked endlessly about their many needs. I thought I had only one need: my husband at my side.

All widows' needs are not the same. Some women rediscover joy and live in contentment by reconstructing their lives with as few changes as possible. Usually they already have in place warm family relations, a network of understanding, compassionate friends, and a strong, caring church fellowship. A stable financial situation is needed to ensure a minimum of disruption.

Other women find it impossible to live their same life pattern without their husbands. Their altered state, in the same setting, causes anxiety. Restlessness, boredom, and lack of direction often mark their lives. They may have no clear picture of what they want their lives to be. This is a danger point if escape mechanisms come into play, and terrible decisions are made. For example, excessive drinking may begin or impulsive intimate relationships may occur. Depression is almost a given at this point, and a characteristic cry is, "I am too tired to deal with this; I don't even know how to make it better."

A widow's needs will never be met unless she defines them to *herself*, and then musters the courage to act on them. She may want to HAVE them fulfilled; she longs for a passive resolution to her pain and confusion. The hard, cold fact is that she will find little satisfaction with her old way of living. This stage of widowhood can result in an exciting inventory of options and decisions. She may gain a new appreciation for who she is and what she can do. This can mark the beginning of a new adventure.

EVENT TIME VERSUS CLOCK TIME

Time seemed divorced from the clock and calendar. I live in a constant state of triage, tending only to emergencies.

At some unobservable and undeniable moment, a widow's life is no longer lived by clock time, but rather by event time. If she must work outside the home, her schedule is built on the necessary events in her life: going to work, getting children off to school, attending soccer games, etc. She does not fit events into her schedule. The events drive her and mandate her schedule. The widow's energy level is diminished, and few things excite her or have much appeal. Therefore, she often opts to do just the absolutely necessary tasks, leaving most other matters undone.

"I thought I was doing well, recovering, getting back to normal. My life had been reduced to manageable bits and pieces strung together by necessity. I awoke at the same time each day, ate the same breakfast, handled my job efficiently. Thought processes were returning to normal. My co-workers allowed me to hide my feelings in my routine work schedule. Having to interact with people all day left me drained; I was eager to go home. Being alone was becoming a welcome relief. Another widow and I were talking about taking a short trip. I was encouraged.

"Then the hail storm battered my roof, sending a waterfall into the den. I was faced with massive repairs. Even though insurance covered most of the damage, I was faced with endless decisions. Did I want to change the color of the walls, what kind of carpet, recover the sofa or buy a new one? I was suddenly angry at my husband for dying, and completely overwhelmed by the whole process. I wanted to cry, to run away, to give up. I tried talking to my children, but they only countered with all the problems they were facing.

"I wanted to scream at the workmen, to tell them to leave…to get out of my sight…get out of my house. I wanted to be left alone. At the same time, I was terrified of being alone with these decisions…with the mess. I did not want to be a widow; I wanted a husband to share the choices, to protect me from mistakes, to tell me it would be 'all right.' I felt helpless and trapped by responsibilities beyond my power to deal with. I broke out in a rash and missed three days of work.

"I realized the pain and frustration of widowhood was enveloping me. I felt like I was dangling in a spider web; no matter how I fought it, I couldn't escape. *Does the feeling ever completely go away?* I wondered."

SURVIVAL VOICES

I was learning! Life was getting better! I could find at least one little pleasure each day, but I still needed to remember that the dance of widowhood is two steps forward, one step backward.

"The power of a grandchild came as a real surprise. We had been a close family before Bill's death; we always enjoyed our daughter's three children. We looked forward to their month-long visit each summer.

"Megan was six when I was swallowed up by widowhood. That year, I said I could handle only one child at a time. Megan was the oldest, and the first to come. I dreaded her questions about Granddad, which I wasn't sure I could answer, since mere survival seemed to be all I could handle.

"To my utter horror, she brought her pet turtle, which died the first day we were alone together. I didn't know what to do, but Megan did. She asked for a little jewelry box. She colored it with crayons and lined it with a bed of cotton. Quite dry-eyed and matter-of-factly, she rested Thumper in the handcrafted coffin. With a garden trowel, we went outside to dig a hole in the flowerbed, by the yellow rose bush. I had no words to speak over a turtle, but not to worry. Megan preached—to me.

"We sat in the grass, and I watched her deep blue eyes grow serious. I loved each freckle on her sunburned nose. Her little-girl voice was sweet, but almost stern. 'Thumper,' she began, 'It's O.K. Pretty soon the leaves are going to get tired and fall off the trees and get stepped on and raked up, and they won't be here any more. That's the way it is with you, Thumper, but it's O.K. We won't forget you.'

"I had never before cried at a turtle's funeral, but that day we both did—the gentle healing kind of tears that ended with hugs and laughter, and cookies and milk on the back porch."

Another widow shares her story:

"It happens repeatedly. The flu, a stomach virus, or a broken bone can seem to wipe out all progress I have achieved. The feeling of being back to 'square one' becomes all-pervasive.

"It came on slowly—an achy feeling spread over my body. Turning my arms and legs into lead weights, defying quick movement. A dull pain wrapped around my head, stiffening my neck and reddening my eyes. Fever burned my face and sent shivers down my spine. I was not a stranger to such symptoms of a flu-like virus, but I was shocked by the consuming loneliness and panic that grabbed me and shook me to the core of my being.

"I had to do battle with reality for the millionth time. There was no husband to stock my cupboard with chicken soup and my refrigerator with 7-up. No mid-day phone calls to monitor my progress.

"The air-conditioning finally hummed me into fitful sleep. In semi-conscious-ness, I sensed my dog crawling onto the foot of the bed, inching his way closer to me. I reluctantly shook off drowsiness to find his black button eyes staring at me from my husband's pillow. Struggling to sit up, I gathered the little animal into my arms and cried into his fur.

"My tears were not a reflection of my illness, but an acknowledgement of regression. All my positive attitudes, all my hard-won little pleasures, dredged up from my new independence, had evaporated.

"Illness, with it own brand of pain, is always a solitary experience, but to be marooned in the arid desert of loneliness most often results in bouts of depression or waves of panic. The weight of widowhood returns to crush any tantalizing dreams of life again lived in joy. I knew I was wallowing in extreme self-pity, but I also knew I would survive."

SURVIVAL STRATEGIES

I knew if I were going to survive, I had to have plans—even everyday suggestions.

Face being alone and separate, even if others are in the house
Feel free to ask for help
Avoid toxic, angry, or judgmental people who want to control
Dress and go outside each day
Talk to another person daily
Move one's body: vacuum, dust, exercise in small segments
Eat at least one healthy meal each day
Perform only safe tasks that do not exceed one's concentration level
Avoid excessive use of alcohol and prescription drugs
Don't feel guilty when a day passes without thinking of one's husband
Don't be alarmed over large gaps in memory
Try to become interested in one thing daily that is beyond grief
Don't run away from thoughts and feelings
Spend as little money as possible; only pay bills
Do not be alarmed by a change in sleep habits
Watch videos, if insomnia is a problem
Take care of health needs, because grief impacts the immune system
Check windows and doors for adequate locks
Try to maintain family schedule and routines
Hire a baby sitter to allow for quiet time
Share feelings with children, appropriate to their age
Allow others to see your tears

"I WILL STRUGGLE":
STRETCHING

I had looked at death and grief as forces outside myself that had seized me. Gradually,
I realized I had to begin looking within myself for the energy to reshape my life.

The second period of widowhood, a time of "stretching," is often forced on women when the mere necessities of life demand their attention. Some widows have to learn to drive. One woman burned up the motor of her car because she did not add oil for two years.

If other family members are in the house, their needs must be considered. Young children will likely become demanding and insecure in the absence of Dad and the obvious disorientation of Mother. Suddenly, she must assume the daily duties of the missing parent. She must begin to assume his chores, or hire them done. This often includes yard work and a variety of home repairs.

Many widows confess that they have almost no memory of day-to-day activities during the first three months. However, during that time, they had to function, performing simple, unavoidable tasks of living. Their fog and confusion often lifted as they began to take action.

During this period, it is helpful to begin to go beyond necessities, to do familiar things in different ways, reflecting a widow's new role as a single person. Going to a movie or eating in a restaurant alone may be difficult, but this can be a healthy step.

Reentry into the world of couples demands stretching. Many widows make the early commitment to themselves to accept all invitations to familiar social events. However, they are unanimous in admitting the intense pain during the first encounter with couples, no matter how close their former friendship. There is always the empty chair, the missing link.

The closer the relationship, the more activities shared as a couple, the more difficult is the adjustment to suddenly becoming single. If most social activities are related to the husband's work, a large void immediately begins to take shape. Sometimes the husband's best friends, on whom the widow thought she could depend, desert her. In truth, a tie to the husband defined the quality of such a friendship. Once he was gone, the wife becomes a non-entity, a mere passing thought.

In this period of stretching, a widow may encounter the frightening realization that she no longer fits into her former social structure. She may find that her changing income cannot sustain parties and travels. Familiar interests and activities may not appeal to her.

Nevertheless, in this period of change, groundwork is being laid for the future. As the reality of the situation becomes clearer, a crisis decision appears: "Will I merely endure, clinging to the past, or will I struggle toward a new and yet undefined way of being?"

At this point, the widow does not fully understand her struggles. Most often, she is muddling forward in desperation. Many women become "stuck," choosing to avoid pain at all costs, mentally remaining married, half of a couple, rather than exploring new possibilities as a single person.

RE-INVENTION OF SELF

Finally, I realized that the cords of grief, which kept me bound, would not loosen until I tried to break free.

The re-invention of self is a defining, conscious moment that occurs when the widow discovers that she *can* take command of reshaping her life in the present. She alone can begin restructuring her existence according to her own plan. She takes control in a new way and sheds any illusions of past dependence on her husband. No matter how shaky the start, she must believe that she is capable of standing on her own two feet.

She must take command of her life, even though she has limitations. Certainly widowhood has proven that she is vulnerable, yet she has the courage to accept herself as a person with different options. She is free to search for new possibilities.

A shift begins from a sad, deprived, uncoupled individual toward a stronger, more independent person. This may be a gradual development. She cannot hide behind her old image of herself as half of a couple. She does not have a husband to prop her up and provide a safety net.

In marriage, she reached within herself and beyond herself; in widowhood, she is thrown back upon herself. The devastation of widowhood is softened and decreased the more she utilizes her dormant and forgotten talents. If she is only using a few coping skills, her pain will be more intense than if she draws from a wider range of strengths. Thus, her inherent personality characteristics, plus skills learned through life experience, can serve her well.

This shift is not a one-time event, but rather a process stemming from a strange mixture of security and insecurity. Before she can boldly venture forth, she must have a sense of equilibrium, and trust in herself. This comes from confidence that has been developed through encouragement and affirmation given by close family members, neighbors, and friends. However, without a sense of insecurity, many women would simply tunnel into what deceptively appears to be a comfortable nest. A moment of boredom, confusion, or desperation forces an identity crisis. She may look in the mirror with a scream, "O God, who am I?

What am I going to do with the rest of my life?" This dramatic desperation propels her into a search for creative change.

An unconscious development of the self may come with a gentle awakening of possibilities that grow and delight with time. This change occurs so gradually that its beginning may be discernible only in retrospect. A nagging sense of unfulfillment or insecurity may have aroused new, realistic expectations

The re-invention of self is looking at one's life from a different angle. It is the product of careful self-evaluation that leads to self-acceptance. A first step is to revisit personal aspirations she had before marriage. Then comes the question: "What are my strengths? What are my weaknesses? What are my responsibilities? What are the desires of my heart?"

Step two is to create time to explore enough new things until something surfaces that is worth the effort to change old habit patterns. A little facet of life that has gone unnoticed may bubble up, causing new delight. Neglected hobbies may become a new vocation. Hope, vision, and expectations gradually expand.

Even if the woman looks the same, does the same work, lives in the same house, she may have become something more than who she was as a wife.

A STRETCHING VOICE

I was shocked to realize that being with close friends could bring intense pain.

Every attempt to socialize is an important step, even though it may feel like a disaster and bring great pain. Listen to the voice of experience:

"The first time I went back to our supper club was one of the most horrible experiences I had to go through. When it was time to sit down to dinner, there it was…an empty chair beside me. I thought I would die on the spot. My throat closed up; I couldn't eat. I thought I would become sick. When I got home, I cried for hours, moaning that the rest of my life I would be alone.

"Soon I was invited to a large party. People were surprised to see me at that event, but it was easier than the dinner with my close friends. My third outing was to a symphony concert with friends whom I knew less well. I discovered that I had missed listening to classical music. The next day I bought several CD's. I had found a new interest that made my days less miserable.

"I learned that any effort to make life less painful is not wasted. Looking back, I see that whether the event was pleasant or ghastly, or simply O.K., each was helpful. Lots of times I could say, 'I made it; it wasn't so bad.' When you can say, 'I made it through,' you get a little more self-confidence…not a lot, but a little.

FAMILIES: FABULOUS OR FALTERING

My grown children seemed tongue-tied around me. I longed to share memories of their father, but if I cried, they would find a reason to abruptly leave. Had we shielded them from the hard realities of life, and now they cannot look at the aftermath of death?

Families can be a source of great help or sad disappointment. The father's death would seem to draw families closer. However, this does not always happen. Widowhood often brings a disconnection and disengagement with family. The task of the widow is to find new ways to connect and re-connect.

Proximity to family impacts such restructuring. If her children live nearby, a pattern of association has been set, and closeness is more easily maintained. This makes emergency situations more manageable, but there is the danger of creating dependent relationships. Quite often, grown children attempt to make too many decisions for their mother and smother her attempts to claim her own personhood.

One widow declared, "My children do not think I have sense enough to scratch fire from the top of my head!" On the other hand, some sons and daughters become distant and unavailable. Either way, seeds of the emerging family system were buried in the former relationships, even though unperceived at the time.

If children live a considerable distance away, the widow is not part of the fabric of their everyday lives; she is more like a visitor. They may not feel as responsible for providing for her well-being as those who live nearby. She may seem detached, by virtue of distance.

Because her life has changed so drastically, the widow often unconsciously expects her children to sense her needs and restructure their lives to fulfill her void. Yet, it is *her* life, which must be restructured. In contrast, the children, if grown, may be in great pain, but their daily existence is relatively unaltered.

Re-structuring family calls for mutual understanding and compassion, with all parties giving each other their own space and separate timetable to make necessary changes. The absence of judgmentalism is a necessity.

The husband and wife were the center of a family power system. When half of this center is removed, often the dominance shifts to the younger generation. Nonetheless, children of strong, independent parents may be terrified if mother crumbles or becomes needy. The formerly self-sufficient mother is equally terrified by finding herself needy. The children may not have a clue about how to help. Also, they cannot offer much support until they have dealt with their own grief issues.

Open, honest communication must flow between all family members, or resentments on the part of the widow are possible, thus bringing separation instead of closeness.

A powerful matriarchal system can and does emerge, particularly if great wealth is involved, or if a family business is in existence. On the other hand, for financial or health reasons, a widow may have to move in with her son or daughter. Such relocation adds great stress and demands a major shift in family structure.

Younger widows, with small children, have different problems. Their daily schedule and set of rules should be maintained as closely as possible to give children a sense of stability. No matter the age of sons and daughters, a widow's sadness and stress should not be totally hidden. It is healthy to share memories—both good and bad—even if tears, as well as laughter, are elicited.

Many widows have declared that their greatest help came from widowed mothers. An older woman, who has survived the trauma of such an experience, can offer the very best understanding and support.

Money issues can distract or destroy family relationships. Inheritance issues can become extremely divisive, even in seemingly strong families. The amount of money or property involved does not dictate the intensity of conflict. A widow's feelings can be deeply assaulted if her standard of living must be drastically reduced. A reliable, trusted, professional financial advisor can help remove unneeded pressure from family members.

Women who do not have children may gain tremendous strength from a network of brothers, sisters, nieces and nephews, and cousins, as well as friends. If close ties have not been maintained through the years, widows may find the impetus and the time to re-establish meaningful contact. Many widows also have found a powerful extended family within their church congregations.

As in all family matters, love, forgiveness, and open communication can work wonders!

INSIGHTS FROM SEASONED WIDOWS

If I did not cling so fiercely to my children, who would keep me from falling into a black hole of despondency?

QUESTION: What about our relationship with our adult children?

The ANSWERS to this came in a sort of chorus:

"Turn them loose! Set them free! Never, never, never cause them to feel guilty about not including you in the daily activities of their lives." The entire group of widows was fierce about this (maybe too much so?). They said it gave them great satisfaction the first time a child called to offer an outing, and they could say honestly that they had another engagement. They even suggested fibbing if the child's sense of responsibility (burden) needed to be lifted.

"Circumstances can vary," they insisted, "but it is hard for many widows to accept the fact that their children have incredibly complicated and active lives. The kindest thing we can do for our children is to regain our own independence, and encourage them to do likewise.

This surely does not rule out the inescapable fact that our children share our grief more deeply than any other person, as our lives remain bound together. Our gift of love and caring is to release them to be what they can be, without the nagging concern about whether they should be doing more for Mother. Hopefully, it will deepen their sense of appreciation, so when we really need them they will come gladly."

STRETCHING STRATEGIES

I knew I could live again when I could make decisions without trying to envision what my husband would want me to do.

Face old responsibilities in a new way.
Learn to adjust: false expectations can result in depression.
Avoid the victim syndrome.
Come to terms with sexual needs.
Guard against intimate relationships too soon.
Avoid people wanting to take advantage of you.
Do not make irrevocable decisions for a year to 18 months.
Make conscious decisions instead of being driven by emotions.
Find hope, even in small instances.
Laugh again.
See beauty in the world around you.
Realize things often do not get better until a year has passed.
Grieve for what really was, not for what might have been.
Do not glorify the past or the person.
Do not look for the "old normal."
Be open to a "new normal."
Plan something special for birthdays, anniversaries, and holidays.
Buy yourself a nice gift for Christmas and your birthday.
Send 4th of July cards instead of Christmas cards.
Write a note to family members whom you love.
Sort your husband's belongings, if you have not already done so.
Find special pictures of your husband to scatter around the house.
Visit the cemetery, if you have been unable to do so, or go less often if it has become a regular ritual.
Undertake only small tasks that can be finished in a short period of time.
Plan an outing with your children or grandchildren.
Buy a pet, even a gold fish, something to take care of.
Work in the yard.

Walk a block in your neighborhood or one trip around the mall.
Eat a new food.
Share your feeling with your children; listen to their feelings.
Search the library for books on grief.

"I WILL GROW AND CHANGE": MOVING

Little pleasures and a growing sense of accomplishment were coming more often, but waves of guilt would quickly dash my progress.
Did I really have the right to be happy again?

There is not a clear distinction between stretching and moving. Nonetheless, there are subtle differences. Work in the moving stage can be described as "choosing" and "doing." This is the time to act on what a widow already knows. Interests are broadening; simple pleasures are becoming more numerous. The widow is less self-absorbed and relates more openly with others. She now can listen to other people and sympathize with their problems and pain. She can see beyond herself to the world of current events.

Her sense of independence is growing, and this increases her confidence as a person. Her preoccupation with grief diminishes. She is facing her singleness, and is finding a few pluses.

She still experiences deep sadness, but acute pain lessens and is no longer overwhelming. Her grief has not ended, but she understands more about the causes of her pain. Difficult times may come as a surprise, when triggered by little things. Her self-absorption is more focused on self-understanding. She is more centered in self-discovery than self-pity. Issues that surfaced in stretching now become full-blown. She has learned that she must deal with the unfinished business of her former life before she can forge a new life.

She has the opportunity to choose what she wants to retain from the old life, and discard the rest. She may want to stay in the same house, or neighborhood, or city. She may want to retain her same job, and continue the same routine of family and social activities. She may be limited by factors that can't be readily changed without great expense or effort. Nonetheless, she has the opportunity to make radical changes, because she has new freedom to do so. She can pick up abandoned dreams and evaluate aptitudes and talents. This can be an exciting time to explore parts of her life which have been neglected or postponed.

INDICATIONS THAT YOU ARE GETTING BETTER

Hope soared like a bouquet of helium balloons on the day I could list eight indications that I was no longer standing still in a puddle of self-pity.

The first belly laugh.
Movement from living in the past to planning for the future.
Looking forward to something: a trip, party, new dress, visit of a friend.
Awareness of flowers, change of seasons.
Pleasure and meaning found in a book.
Return of the ability to make decisions, even small ones.
Decision to laugh, rather than cry.
Self-confidence bred by new responsibilities handled well.
Owning mistakes without being devastated or feeling husband's censure.

MOVING FORWARD

I had to learn the difference between marching forward in uncharted terrain and plodding endlessly in familiar circles.

"Jerry's death in a motorcycle accident brought an abrupt halt to all movement in my personal world. Every familiar action ceased. Not a comma, a pause mark, but a gigantic period had been dropped in my life. For hours, days, weeks, everything stopped; I was on hold. Not only actions, but also thoughts were immobilized.

"Meaningful, forward momentum was slow in returning and could not be rushed. As I sat in my chair for endless periods of time, I began to envy women who had to return immediately to the demands of family or job. They seemed propelled back into the actions of living, while I was too benumbed to stir.

"However, I now know that everyday action is not necessarily forward movement, but can be merely a circular routine allowing us to become too busy, or not perceptive enough, to know what we must do to really feel alive again.

"I have come a long way beyond just getting through the days. I have had unexpected moments of real pleasure, and I am proud of a few of my solo accomplishments. Yet I still don't know what I must do to become a whole person again. I have allowed myself to have a few vague hopes for the future, but I don't know how to get from 'here' to 'there,' and I am afraid to try."

Just as this widow points out, it is easy to get stuck in the early stages of pain and denial. It is equally possible to become bogged down in the later stages of grief work. When life begins to return to a somewhat pleasant and hopeful experience, dreams and longings are a positive, necessary sign of the renewal process. However, these tantalizingly wonderful ideas and mental pictures of happiness can become monsters to terrorize widows if allowed to remain mere fantasies. Persons remain stuck in the idea stage if they fail to *take action* to bring about the longed-for future.

There is a rhythm to the journey through widowhood. There is a time to be still and introspective, to allow pain to surface, and define it with the new language of grief. There also is a time to take action and initiate movement into new creative life. Just as a language of grief was needed to express pain adequately, a language of hope is necessary to help propel a widow beyond the floating images of the future.

At such times, a widow may think "At last I have come through the tunnel of grief! At last I have experienced a taste of joy. At last I have visions and longings for happiness and creativity!"

Nevertheless, this is the very spot where she may become stuck and spiral into a period of deep inaction and subsequent depression. This can occur when a widow chooses to stay in the safe, hopeful world of merely dreaming of positive experiences. Instead, she must act out her visions and follow her cherished desires. Otherwise, her dreams will mock her, and she will regress to a previous state of lethargy.

A widow must begin to live again, abandoning an assortment of fears: fear of the unknown, fear of the new and different, fear of the untried, fear of what family, friends, and co-workers might think of her. Then she can dare to move in new directions and do things which may seem "uncharacteristic" of her. It is in the "doing" that she gains new strengths, new joy and new meaning—virtually a new life!

Grasping and actualizing this newness is necessary, because widowhood has changed her. Now she must change her life. Whether she has been willing to take part in the change and reinvent herself, or whether she allowed circumstances to roll over her, she is, nonetheless, quite different from the person she was when her husband was alive. Acknowledgment of that fact is vital; exploration of that fact is life-giving.

MOVING VOICES

Little seeds of hope grew into miracles of healing
when I listened to others share their stories.

One survivor of 60 years of marriage, followed by five years of widowhood, announced that she has changed so much her husband would hardly recognize her. With a smile and a twinkle in her eyes, she added, "I think he would like me even more now. I have to admit I have had great success, taking over management of a farm and a housing development. George had always talked business with me, but my personal domain had never spilled beyond household duties. I am really proud of abilities I did not know I even possessed."

Another widow shares her experience:

"The woman across the aisle on the plane looked vaguely familiar. I noticed her in an absent-minded sort of way when I put my bag in the overhead bin. It was my first business trip after Jack's death. I felt so "different" from everyone else; I imagined myself an alien. I was sure people around me could read the deep sorrow and confusion that I felt. I honestly thought I was cosmetically altered by my grief.

"I buckled my seat belt and closed my eyes, hoping I could squeeze out the babble of voices around me. I heard someone say, 'Don't I know you?' I didn't think anyone would dare break through my obvious retreat into myself. I did not open my eyes until I felt a hand reach across the aisle and tug at my sleeve.

"There was Kaye, my suite-mate from college. The same smile lit up her face; she was delighted to recognize me after 15 years. The seat next to her was empty, and she literally pulled me across the aisle. Actually she pulled me across some invisible line of self-pity.

"She, too, was a widow; her husband had been killed in a private plane crash seven years ago. I asked how she had the courage to fly. She began to tell me of agonizing episodes of facing down her fears, and not being afraid to ask for help. Our two-hour plane ride was too short. We promised to stay in touch through e-mail. For a long time, I had a brief, daily word of challenge on my computer screen each morning at work. She taught me how to be 'an evangelist of hope,' reaching beyond fear and self-obsession. Eventually, I started a widow's group at my church.

"I wonder if that business trip was a coincidence? It certainly changed my life."

MOVING STRATEGIES

Sitting on the retaining wall at the lake, with my feet splashing in the water, I began to list possibilities for the future. For the first time, I could picture my life with happy anticipation.

A group of widows shared their strategies for moving forward with their lives:
Create a new tradition for holidays.
Renew a friendship.
Plan a trip at an otherwise sad time of the year.
Learn something new, perhaps computer skills.
List three postponed dreams.
Seriously explore the possibility of one dream.
Redecorate the master bedroom.
Compile a family album for the children.
Volunteer at a hospital, nursing home or church.
Take a friend to lunch at a new or different restaurant.
Begin to explore the desirability of a different residence.
Participate in mentally stimulating activities, such as a library book club.
Do needlework, play the piano, write a letter.
Do memory work or crossword puzzles.

SPECIAL REWARDS FOR SMALL FEATS

I felt so good after I mowed the lawn for the first time! I cut all the blossoms off my husband's prize rose bushes, and filled every vase in the house—something he would never let me do!

Reward yourself when you alone have accomplished some difficult task. Celebration may be in order for something as small as the first time you have taken the car for an oil change, or for something as monumental as buying a new car.

Reward yourself when you manage to endure the first painful holidays or other sentimental dates on your calendar.

Reward yourself when you use new skills or old talents. You may discover for the first time that you can knit or do needlepoint, or you may find time to regain the old joy of line dancing or tennis.

The rewards should be small pleasures or mini-extravagances that help a person feel good about herself. After hours poring over bank statements, the account is reconciled! The treat of an extra long soak in a bubble bath may be a fitting reward. When all the thank you notes are in the mail, buy a small bunch of cut-flowers for the breakfast room table. Wait to purchase a much wanted paperback novel until some dreaded problem has been dealt with.

Rewards may be as simple as positive thoughts. When self-permission has been granted to shed tears that have been bottled up for weeks, a fine reward is the sweet affirmation that something healthy has been done.

OLD COMPASS
NEW COMPASS

OLD COMPASS

Notice all empty holes in your life
Escape reality
Sink into sadness
Waste time with wishful thinking

NEW COMPASS

Nourish your faith
Evaluate your strengths and interests
Surround yourself with positives
Work toward a specific written goal

FAITH: A LIFE AND DEATH MATTER

I believe, O God—but help my unbelief.

Scripture proclaims:

We do not lose heart. Even though our outer nature is wasting away, our inner nature is being renewed day by day. For this slight momentary affliction is preparing us for an eternal weight of glory beyond all measure, because we look not at what can be seen but at what cannot be seen; for what can be seen is temporary, but what cannot be seen is eternal.

For we know that if the earthly tent we live in is destroyed, we have a building from God, a house not made with hands, eternal in the heavens. For in this tent we groan, longing to be clothed with our heavenly dwelling—if indeed, when we have taken it off we will not be found naked. For while we are still in this tent, we groan under our burden, because we wish not to be unclothed but to be further clothed, so that what is mortal may be swallowed up by life. He who has prepared us for this very thing is God, who has given us the Spirit as a guarantee.

So we are always confident; even though we know that while we are at home in the body we are away from the Lord—for we walk by faith, not by sight." 2 Corinthians 4:16-5:7

Life and death, in their essence, are shrouded in mystery, yet every religion known to humankind endeavors to make sense out of living and dying. Certain marker events in the lives of individuals catapult them into this quest for understanding. The death of a spouse can be one such catalyst.

Loss and pain dull understanding, while at the same time rouse deep questions and longings. Unfortunately, the depths of life and death matters are most often discussed in metaphoric terms, such as "the valley of the shadow of death." This is both puzzling and frustrating for the widow who demands to know where heaven is, what it is like, and what her husband is doing there. These questions are not unusual, because the present information explosion that causes society to expect a provable answer to every question intensifies the demand for literal answers.

The mystery of death defies this glut of computerized knowledge and begins to unravel in the light of Scripture and the power of faith.

VOICES OF THE FAITHFUL

In the midst of my agony, God met me, and called me back to faith.

A widow shares her spiritual journey:

"My faith experience is going to sound really weird! We never thought much about religion, except occasionally on Easter Sunday. Our next-door neighbor certainly tried to get us interested in her church. I guess, if asked, we would have acknowledged the existence of God, but this didn't seem important to us at the time. Harrison was a police officer, and the chaplain on the force conducted his funeral.

"My neighbor brought me a casserole and a purple African violet that spilled blooms over the tiny clay pot. I was glad she did not talk to me about religion. I put the plant on a windowsill and forgot all about it. A week later, I noticed the pitiful thing with dead blooms and limp leaves. I intended to pitch it in the trash, but instead I sloshed water over it from the glass I was holding in my hand.

"Weeks later, I noticed the plant was not dead, but actually blooming again! I was so amazed, I put it on my breakfast table. I marveled at its resilience. I thought, *this is a miracle, a resurrection.*

"I kept thinking about the plant, and for some reason—which I don't understand—I went to a church supper with my neighbor, and then a grief seminar there, and before I knew it, I was attending Sunday School. I am still not sure about God, but the worship service is beautiful, and the hymns comfort me.

"My sense of loss and grief have not lessened, but I am beginning to glimpse death as a new beginning, not an end. Hope and peace are not just words; they are realities which I am learning to hang onto.

"I can't get away from the question: 'Did God touch me through that little violet plant?' Maybe I'll know someday!"

Another widow explains:

"At times, I seemed to be in constant conversation with God. I can't call it prayer…there were no formal words of praise or thanksgiving. I just mumbled words: 'God, get me through the day,' or 'God, help me with these bank statements; I can't reconcile them,' or 'Help me know whether to get a new car or repair my old one.' If this was really prayer, it was an automatic response of heart and mind.

"I told a well-meaning friend about this. She chided me, saying I should reserve prayer for more important matters, and I should be more respectfully formal. I finally talked to my pastor, who explained that prayer can be a personal relationship, not merely a stylized verbal recitation. He helped me understand that I can pray with my thoughts, and at times when I don't know what to pray for.

"Every day for months I read Romans 8:26: *The Spirit helps us in our weakness; for we do not know how to pray as we ought, but that very Spirit intercedes with sighs too deep for words.*

"My church attendance is still irregular, but I don't know how I would have survived my husband's loss without reaching out to God."

VOICES OF SCRIPTURE

Do not let your hearts be troubled. Believe in God, believe also in me. In my Father's house there are many dwelling places. If it were not so, would I have told you that I go to prepare a place for you? And if I go and prepare a place for you, I will come again and will take you to myself, so that where I am, there you may be also. And you know the way to the place where I am going. Thomas said to him, "Lord, we do not know where you are going. How can we know the way?" Jesus said to him, "I am the way, and the truth, and the life." John 14:1-6

I will not leave you orphaned; I am coming to you. In a little while the world will no longer see me, but you will see me; because I live, you also will live. On that day you will know that I am in my Father, and you in me, and I in you. They who have my commandments and keep them are those who love me; and those who love me will be loved by my Father, and I will love them and reveal myself to them." John 14:18-21

No, in all these things we are more than conquerors through him who loved us. For I am convinced that neither death, nor life, nor angels, nor rulers, nor things present, nor things to come, nor powers, nor height, nor depth, nor anything else in all creation, will be able to separate us from the love of God in Christ Jesus our Lord. Romans 8:37-39

Why are you cast down, O my soul,
and why are you disquieted within me?
Hope in God; for I shall again praise him,
my help and my God." Psalm 43:5

The Lord is my shepherd, I shall not want.
He makes me lie down in green pastures;
he leads me beside still waters;

he restores my soul.
He leads me in right paths for his name's sake.
Even though I walk through the darkest valley,
I fear no evil;
for you are with me;
your rod and your staff—they comfort me.
You prepare a table before me
in the presence of my enemies;
you anoint my head with oil;
my cup overflows.
Surely goodness and mercy shall follow me
all the days of my life,
and I shall dwell in the house of the Lord my whole life long.
Psalm 23

May you be made strong with all the strength that comes from his glorious power, and may you be prepared to endure everything with patience, while joyfully giving thanks to the Father, who has enabled you to share in the inheritance of the saints in the light. He has rescued us from the power of darkness and transferred us into the kingdom of his beloved Son, in whom we have redemption, the forgiveness of sins.

Colossians 1:11-14

PRAYER OF CHANGE

I knew I had to reach beyond myself if my life was ever to have meaning.

Ever loving God, so many times I did not think I could make it through another day of pain and emptiness. But somehow I have survived! You must have held me in love, even when I thought you were too far away to care.

Thank you for the times that I have actually laughed. Thank you for giving me strength to make a few decisions.

When I was numb with grief, I was not as fearful as I am today. Please help me pick up the pieces of my life and become some sort of whole person again.

Help me to be able to see beyond my own hurting. Help me to understand that other members of the family are hurting in different ways. Help me not to judge harshly those family and friends who do not even see my aching needs.

O God, prayer is just as jumbled as my mind, but at least I claim some words to try to sound out the fear and hope that battle in my soul.

PART III

RE-DISCOVERING JOY

JOY VERSUS HAPPINESS

Weeping may linger for the night but joy comes with the morning.
Psalm 30:5

Joy is recognition of a buoyant sense of well-being. It is a deep satisfaction, which permeates the entire person. Joy is the great liberator. Out of nowhere, a sparkling moment of delight pierces the darkness of grief. An unexpected experience of pure pleasure animates life once again.

Joy often comes as a surprise, bringing a rush of bubbly pleasure. At other times joy comes with a quiet, gentle embrace. In delight, the widow acknowledges, "This is really good!"

Happiness is a part of joy, as breath is a part of life. Life is much more than breath; joy is much more than happiness. Joy is an internal experience that comes as a gift, whereas happiness is dependent on external circumstances, and can be worked for.

Joy and happiness share many similarities, but they also differ in significant ways. For example, they both are pleasurable emotions, experienced with deep feelings; both are desirable. They lighten the mood and generate energy. Both can be fleeting and episodic, but joy has a longer after-glow, leading to the hope that such a life-giving experience can occur again. Joy satisfies at a deeper level of consciousness than happiness.

Joy is like receiving an unexpected year-end bonus; happiness is more like earning a generous hourly wage. Joy is personal and inexplicable, while happiness is more gregarious and definable.

Joy may not be tied to expectations, while happiness usually is. Therefore, the source of happiness is readily apparent, being connected to concrete events. Joy transcends circumstances. Joy can be experienced in the midst of deep sorrow, but happiness cannot.

Joy includes a sense of well-being, even in the midst of difficulty; a spirit of optimism, even in the midst of uncertainty. Joy can propel one into activity. Even if the body is somewhat disabled, activity of mind can lead to a new and enriched quality of life.

Joy does not change the pain and burden of widowhood, but it does transform the routines of daily life. Joy is contagious, and it can bring stability to stressed relationships. Joy has a calming effect on family and friends who may be bewildered by the many manifestations of grief.

Joy, even in the smallest measure, is a signal that life can become manageable again, and that purpose and resolve can give birth to tangible events and future plans. Joy shortens time and lengthens pleasure.

Joy is as hard to grasp as a fistful of air. There are no do-it-yourself manuals for the achievement of joy. Instead, it can be received inwardly, accepted, almost absorbed from the rhythm of life itself.

Joy can be experienced with excitement and anticipation. This is important for the widow. After a few experiences of joy, she often begins to look for positive signs in her life, thus shifting her consciousness away from her pain. Joy awakens forgotten feelings of vitality. This gives a widow hope that she is not dead inside, but is alive again.

For every gift there must be a giver. In the case of joy, the giver is often elusive and hidden. Joy is a gift that love bestows. To receive love, one must be willing to experience sorrow, as well as happiness. Love softens minds and hearts and allows the solitary center of an individual to be touched by another human being, and ultimately by God. Someone more important, more precious, more wonderful than self is cherished, and in so doing, the core of one's self is cracked open and can, at last, receive and acknowledge joy.

A widow's loss and pain destroy happiness for a time, but deepen the wellspring from which joy can return. Even in the bleakest moments of life, the capacity to receive moments of joy is never lost.

JOY BLOCKERS

As a starving person craves food, I hungered for deep-seated laughter to shake loose specks of morbidity clinging to my thoughts, but I could not create joy any more than I could create flowers out of ashes.

Joy is a free agent; however, the reception of joy can be blocked by feelings of:

Bitterness
Anger
Worry
Fear
Anxiety
Low self esteem
Guilt
Obsession with the past
Pessimism
Self absorption
Depression
Unforgiving spirit

It is not uncommon for a woman to experience many of these feelings in widowhood. Brief moments of joy can break through almost any barrier. Some people are so bitter that joy has little chance. However, If blockers are faced and eliminated, moments of joy multiply, and fresh visions of hope appear.

JOY MAGNETS

Sitting in a closed-up house, I could not enjoy the freshness of Spring until I opened a window to its breezes. I could not draw in the energy of joy until I opened myself to its possibilities.

Although joy cannot be created by personal effort, there are conditions that make reception of joy a greater possibility. These include:

A sense of awe
Life in the present
Uncluttered thoughts
Quiet time
Stillness of spirit
Meditation
Worship
Prayer
Appreciation of

Music
Art
Literature
Nature

Openness to the future
Journaling

BOGUS JOYS

Traveling through widowhood is sometimes like crawling through a minefield where false pleasures explode with startling force.

In an effort to fill the void in her life, a widow may foolishly grasp for shallow pleasures and quick diversions, such as:

Aimless activities
Money
Possessions
Expensive cars
New wardrobe
Latest gadgets
Different house
Status
Sex
Food
Alcohol
Excessive medication

JOY: THE EXQUISITE GIFT

All my life I had experienced joy as part of my birthright. Now I welcome joy as an unmerited treasure.

Widowhood often begins as a disengagement with life that seems too foreign and complex, too empty and dismal, to embrace. Life has become brittle, and time becomes frozen in immutable dread. Yet surprising little moments of joy can come early in a widow's struggle, offering a glimmer of hope for a future too distant to have form and shape. Minute and fleeting, these experiences may hardly be recognizable. They may only be seeds of promise sown almost secretly in the fallow ground of heartache.

Finally, a moment of joy breaks through the dense fog of grief: the first spontaneous, out-loud laugh, lingering in mind and heart; the breathtaking fire of autumn colors burning away self-absorption, demanding full attention; the return of taste and substance to food, seasoned with the compassion of a friend who can sit silently through times of wordless pain.

This first joy may come with a shock and a jolt, piercing through a long period of numbness. Nonetheless, the return of joy is often the first step back to a life of normalcy. Joys, no matter how small, are like shocking an injured heart back into rhythm. Such experiences are not quickly forgotten. They deeply imprint memory with thoughts that can be relived repeatedly, adding a glimmer of hope with each return visit.

Joy is not an experience that can be shared adequately with another person. The end product can be seen, and feelings can be described, but the essence of joy resides deep within the individual. Yet joy is an "Aha!" that transcends the self. At least for a moment, pain, impossibilities, personal preoccupation is blown away by a sparkling delight, or by a quiet assurance that reshapes hopelessness into promise.

The natural response is to want to hug moments of joy to one's self and hold onto them; but that is impossible, because by nature, joy is fleeting. Nonetheless, recognizing and savoring everyday, ordinary joys can lead to a positive attitude toward life. Joy leads to the certain hope and the unwavering trust that life has a purpose and pattern. Joy leads to expectancy. Joy begets coping skills. Joy becomes a lens through which we view life.

To plumb the depths of joy, it is necessary to transform fear of aloneness into a warm acceptance of solitude. Constant agitation and unending busyness rob one of wisdom, which joy offers. Joy remains merely a pleasurable sensation unless we are still and quiet enough to meditate on its meaning, to be led by its direction. For instance, joy comes as a gift. Who is the gift-giver, or from what source does it emanate? Joy rides on the back of hope. From where does hope come? Such a search is as ancient as time itself, and the quest seems indelibly imprinted on our minds and spirits. Centuries-old words stir in grief-churned thoughts:

My help comes from the Lord, who made heaven and earth.
Psalm 121:2

VOICES OF JOY

Joy can come as a whispered aria of love or as a thunderous symphony of celebration. Either way, it makes the dance of life worthwhile.

A widow explains:

"When joy returns, it is like finding a lifejacket when the boat is sinking! I felt that life would never have meaning again. I had spent months going through the same routine, one dragging day after another. Walking the dog was a regular escape maneuver. One day, for some unplanned reason, I varied our route, and we crossed over a little neighborhood creek.

"I stopped on the bridge to watch a mother duck swim by, with three plump, yellow ducklings splashing behind her. I distinctly remember feeling a smile spread over my face. Tension in my body began to ease; I was aware of the sun warming my face. I suddenly realized that Spring had come, without my notice. In some mysterious way, I knew that my feelings, frozen by grief, would thaw, and I would be alive again. Looking back, I realize that was a moment of pure joy; a gift bestowed upon me."

Another widow tells her story:

"For me, the first experience of joy came when I was able to help someone who was in worse condition than I was. A long-time friend had had a stroke. I visited her because I knew I should; no big deal. However, I was overwhelmed by how much pleasure she derived from our time together. She made me feel appreciated and valued. No doubt about it; she gifted me with joy! So often, I find the focus of joy comes from beyond myself."

A third widow gives testimony to joy:

"The possibility of inner pleasure became a source of joy. However, I began to agonize over the question, 'Do I have the right to feel such deep satisfaction when my precious husband is gone?' Finally I confided my fears to a close friend, who helped me understand that the return of joy is among the first signs of making it through the tunnel of grief. It was like going from darkness to light!"

Another widow shares her feelings:

"The party at Mary's lake house was a turning point in my life. I didn't realize it at the time, but looking back I understand how important it was. I hadn't wanted to go. I had made all sorts of excuses. I simply wasn't ready for a weekend away from home, not even a year after Steve's death. Finally, I knew Mary would not let me say 'no'.

"Two couples and I were invited. I thought it would be awkward, but everyone was so relaxed and caring, soon I forgot I was a single person amid couples.

"I got up early Sunday to watch the sunrise. The beauty of daylight robbing the night of darkness spoke to me with wordless beauty. I sat alone on the deck, drinking coffee, and for the first time in all those long, horrible months, I was aware of a deep feeling of well-being. I was surprised by the peace of the moment which stilled my morbid thoughts and lifted me out of myself. I could feel the love and concern of my still-sleeping friends. I was actually hungry for breakfast. I guess it was a moment of real joy, to be celebrated with thanksgiving. I reasoned that if I felt that way once, maybe I would again."

DECLARATIONS OF JOY

The negative forces of widowhood were being diminished ever so slightly by the positive charge of joy.

Joy is one of life's most positive emotions.

Joy expands a woman's life.

Joy gives a respite from sadness.

Joy lifts the spirit.

Joy clears one's vision.

Joy releases tension.

Joy provides a new way of looking at ordinary things.

Joy imprints memory.

Joy intertwines with love.

Joy offers a lens through which we view life.

Joy bestows hope and trust.

Joy begets coping skills.

Joy leads to laughter.

Joy brings new life.

Joy mellows into contentment.

FAITH: A SHOUT OF JOY

"You show me the path of life. In your presence is the fullness of joy"
Psalm 16:11

Joy is the natural response to any personal revelation of God's presence and love. The breathtaking surprise of joy amid pain can mark a pathway to God, who has promised in Psalm 126 that *"those who sow in tears, shall reap in joy."*

The word joy and its derivatives occur more than 200 times in the Bible. Joy can feed faith and heal brokenness. Religious experiences that point beyond self open up new possibilities for bursts of delight that loosen the grip of grief.

A jubilant song of faith for the widow to grasp is best captured by the poetic words of Psalm 5:11, found in the King James Version of the Bible: *"Let all those who put their trust in thee rejoice; let them ever shout with joy because thou defendest them; let them also that love thy name be joyful in thee."* A picture of God's power met with human trust emerges. Joy becomes a manifestation of faith.

It is right to pray for joy if the petition is prompted by a worthy motive: not joy for joy's sake, but rather for the reconnection to God and God's grace, which guarantees joy. Thus the Psalmist cries *"Restore to me the joy of my salvation,"* Psalm 51:12. The yearning of the Psalmist's heart can infuse the widow with determination to break free of grief and rebuild a strong life of faith.

On the night Jesus was born, shepherds "were overwhelmed with joy" when a band of angels announced the Savior's birth. The power of their unutterable joy was part of the energy that sped them through the sleeping town to the holy stable.

Perhaps the Apostle Paul best explained joy when he prayed, *"May the God of hope fill you with all joy and peace in believing, so that you may abound in hope by the power of the Holy Spirit,"* Romans 15:13.

The experience of joy and hope can become a solid foundation for a widow's redefined life of peace and contentment. Helen Keller declared, "Joy is the holy fire that keeps our purpose warm and our intelligence aglow."

JOY IN SCRIPTURE

Do not fear, for I have redeemed you;
I have called you by name, you are mine.
When you pass through the waters, I will be with you;
and through the rivers, they shall not overwhelm you;
when you walk through fire you shall not be burned,
and the flame shall not consume you.
For I am the Lord your God. Isaiah 43:1-3

I waited patiently for the Lord;
he inclined to me and heard my cry.
He drew me up from the desolate pit,
out of the miry bog,
and set my feet upon a rock, making my steps secure.
He put a new song in my mouth,
a song of praise to our God.
Psalm 40:1-3

Clap your hands, all you peoples;
shout to God with loud songs of joy. Psalm 47:1

Be merciful to me, O God, be merciful to me,
for in you my soul takes refuge;
in the shadow of your wings I will take refuge,
until the destroying storms pass by.
I cry to God Most High,
to God who fulfills his purpose for me. Psalm 57:1-2

Blessed be the Lord, who daily bears us up;
God is our salvation. Psalm 68:19

Make a joyful noise to the Lord, all the earth.
Worship the Lord with gladness;
come into his presence with singing.
Know that the Lord is God.
It is he that made us, and we are his;
we are his people, and the sheep of his pasture.
Enter his gates with thanksgiving,
and his courts with praise.
Give thanks to him, bless his name.
For the Lord is good;
his steadfast love endures forever,
and his faithfulness to all generations. Psalm 100

Then they cried to the Lord in their trouble,
and he saved them from their distress;
he sent out his word and healed them,
and delivered them from destruction.
Let them thank the Lord for his steadfast love,
for his wonderful works to humankind.
And let them offer thanksgiving sacrifices,
and tell of his deeds with songs of joy. Psalm 107:19b-22

I rise before dawn and cry for help;
I put my hope in your words. Psalm 119:147

Rejoice in the Lord always; again I will say, Rejoice. Let your gentleness be known to everyone. The Lord is near. Do not worry about anything, but in everything by prayer and supplication with thanksgiving let your requests be made known to God. And the peace of God, which surpasses all understanding, will guard your hearts and your minds in Christ Jesus. Finally, beloved, whatever is true, whatever is honorable, whatever is just, whatever is pure, whatever is pleasing, whatever is commendable, if there is any excellence and if there is anything worthy of praise, think about these things. Keep on doing the things that you have learned and received and heard and seen in me, and the God of peace will be with you. Philippians 4:4-9

PRAYER OF JOY

O God, you are the worker of major miracles through tiny everyday happenings. My words cannot contain the thanksgivings I offer to you! Still clinging to my shroud of grief, I thought I would never experience joy again, but you sent me moments of delight in a crimson sunset, in trees dressed in golden fall foliage, in the antics of children.

I never thought I would laugh again, but I am beginning to find merriment all around me. My forced smiles are becoming hardy chuckles that feel so good! Yet delight is often followed by waves of guilt: how can I feel so good when my husband is dead? Lord, help me sort out my conflicting emotions. I know he would not want me mired in misery; but my mind and heart are out of sync.

Forgive me for taking my family and friends for granted. I treasure each one, and pray your blessing on them. Meet each one at the cutting edge of their deepest needs.

You have given me strength that I didn't know I had; I am ready to take baby steps into the future. I have let my own pain and neediness drain everyone around me. Forgive me. Now I want to be a conduit of your love to them.

Please accept these rambling words, because I am just now climbing out of the pit of self-absorption. I am still shaky, but your world is so full of beauty, and life is good again. O God, I am so full of gratitude and thankfulness! A thousand times I want to shout, Thank you! Thank you! Amen.

PART IV
LIVING IN CONTENTMENT

CONTENTMENT DEFINED

Finally I was able to sustain whole days of quiet satisfaction with life in general.

Contentment is a relaxed state of being that reaches beyond a grudging tolerance of life. Contentment is sustained by anticipation and hope. It is a place to store open-ended expectations.

Contentment is living under the promise of joy. Every moment is not hilarious or joy-filled. However, the reflections of joy color the most average and ordinary events.

In the realm of contentment, successes and failures do not precipitate extreme highs and lows, but are tolerated as a genuine part of life. Grief has not been eradicated, but rather tamed. Sadness still can wreak havoc at strange, unexpected moments. Counsel and compassionate understanding may still be needed from time to time. In contentment, the variables in life do not threaten ruin; the constants in life sustain harmony and fuel hope.

Personal expectations are realistic. Plans for the future are more challenging than frightening. New experiences are sought with delight. The widow finally has moved beyond the confines of her small world of self, and now is able to reach out to others in love.

The old saying becomes acceptable: "God is in his heaven and all is right with her world"—at least *most* of the time. When doubts threaten to paralyze, a litany of affirmation has been lived through and stands ready to encourage new vitality.

A PLATEAU OF PEACE

The imprint of grief no longer mars every day. I am finding more peace than pain, more pleasure than fear, more purpose than rootlessness.

A plateau is a level place where a period or condition of stability is possible.

A widow reaches a plateau of peace when she accepts contentment, rather than happiness, as a goal in life. Happiness is episodic, while contentment is more sustainable, though not unbroken. The widow can experience a growing satisfaction with her possessions, status, and life in general. In fact, life can be declared good, *very* good.

The tension of grief has lessened; memories bless rather than burn. The past is neither closed off nor worshipped. The future is neither an obsession nor a preoccupation. The widow can reach beyond thoughts of herself. Emotions are controlled or freely expressed, whichever is appropriate.

Now she is ready to both receive and give love. This state of contentment, of being at peace with herself, is a prerequisite to forming intimate relationships or entertaining thoughts of remarriage.

A widow shares her experience:

"I thought I could not live without a man in my life. I grieved deeply for Stan. Our marriage had been wonderful and exciting, but I felt so fractured and incomplete without a male presence. I desperately longed for happiness I had found only in marriage. I scrutinized every man I met, and meticulously graded him as a possible mate.

"Now I realize in the early stages of grief, I was looking for almost any man to fill that awful void. Now, after finding pleasure in being who I am today, I am no longer desperate, and I know I need an equal partner, rather than someone I might imagine as a rescuing Prince Charming. I had to reach a degree of personal or inner satisfaction before I was ready to form any kind of sustained relationship."

DAILY LIVING ON LEVEL GROUND

I had not totally conquered sadness, but it was receding into the background of busy, pleasurable days. I was even looking forward to the future with newfound confidence.

A widow reaches level ground when she has climbed out of the bottomless pit of grief. She now can live most days with a sense of equilibrium, regaining a sense of delight and developing a spirit of serenity. She awakens on most days with a feeling of pleasure, as she plans the hours ahead. She anticipates gentle happiness and revels in simple accomplishments. Joy is often experienced, and laughter comes easily. She has carved out a comfortable routine which includes private time for herself, as well as a social time for family and friends. She initiates plans with others.

The widow finds herself increasingly capable of handling daily annoyances and everyday problems. She is aware of her strengths and weaknesses, and will freely address either. She refuses to glorify the past or wildly fantasize about the future. She is well-grounded in the present. She gives herself permission to choose carefully the people with whom she shares her life and the events into which she will pour her energy. She can be a caregiver more often than a care receiver.

She may find this plateau deeply satisfying, and decide to remain there the rest of her life. On the other hand, new interests or unforeseen crises may lead her to struggle toward yet undreamed-of adventure or feats of heroic endurance.

A plateau of peace can be a place of necessary respite to be visited and re-visited, or it can be a home of sanctuary and grace.

20–20 VISION

I was no longer afraid of life; I knew I was a survivor.

To move into a productive, satisfying future, a widow must exercise 20-20 vision. She must live within the confines of reality, seeing the present as it really is, not as it used to be, or perhaps could have been.

By now, financial resources must be clearly understood and utilized. Debts must be tallied along with assets. Earnings, savings, and spending must be in balance.

Health issues must be faced. Proper diet and appropriate exercise need to be maintained.

Personal aptitudes and skills should be explored anew. The possibility of continuing education can be assessed in the process of self-discovery. To either minimize or inflate one's abilities usually leads to disillusionment or depression.

Trusted, supportive friends and family members must be appreciated and thanked. Those from whom attention and care were lacking must be forgiven, so the widow can be released from feelings of bitterness and disappointment.

Contentment is based on truth recognized and reality accepted.

HOME SWEET HOME

I surprised myself with the determination and strength not only to build a new life, but also to build a new container for my life: a new house.

A widow shares pages from her diary:

"Sometimes you have to be alone in a house before it becomes your own. You have to talk to it, and let it talk to you. You have to walk through it early in the morning and late at night. You have to raise and lower all the blinds, open the shutters, turn off and on lights, stand still and scrutinize the view from each window.

"You have to take an inventory of activities that may possibly occur in each room, and arrange and rearrange the furniture accordingly. It is best to sparsely furnish the house at first; let sofas and chairs, lamps and tables arrive as life begins to unfold there.

"Bonding of person to house requires lots of quiet listening. Relish the wind as it whispers through the trees, rattles the ivy that climbs on the wall under the bathroom window, and screams around the corners of the house. I have done all of that, and now I feel at home in my newly structured life, in my newly built house."

VOICES OF CONTENTMENT

As I had once gained strength from the stories of other widows, I could now share in their blessed affirmations of life.

A widow tells her story:

"I was determined to survive through the skids of grief—the times when events or memories would send me out of control, crashing into a spiral of depression with fits of sadness and days of irrepressible tears. I would think that I had overcome those involuntary reactions, but there I would be, caught in a frantic dance of grief: three steps forward, and two backward.

"Finally, I discovered history was my best ally. When enough time had passed, I could look back and recall how I had gotten through other rough times and realize that I could do it again."

Another widow explains:

"Bob is dead and gone, and I hate to say it out loud, but it is the truth: he was mean. I would never have divorced him, but his constant criticism and nagging manner made my very existence miserable. He was domineering and down right disgusting at times.

"For the first time in twenty-nine years, I have time and money to take care of myself. I sometimes feel guilty for being so contented, so at peace with myself and the world."

A third widow explains her contentment:

"I reached for a book on the top shelf of the book case, and a picture of Ted fluttered down. It was taken on our last vacation trip together. Ted was smiling up at me from the little scrap of paper at my feet.

"For a moment, my heart beat faster and I was thrilled. I sat on the floor and looked at it, as if I expected the photo to have a voice and speak to me. And I guess, in truth it did, because a wealth of joyful memories washed over me. I remembered with delight that day long years ago! I could almost feel the Italian sunshine that warmed us as we sat on a hillside having a picnic, just the two of us.

114

"If I had found the photograph a year or so after my husband's death, I would have been stabbed with aching loneliness and pain. But discovering it so suddenly, after 5 years of widowhood, was a joyful experience. It was a reminder that Ted will always be a part of who I am. It made me feel stronger, really—thankful that we had two decades together.

"Since I am finding pleasure in my life today, reminders of past joys are not sad, rather they are reassuring that life is more than the past; it is a whole, with the present and the future taking turns to satisfy me.

"I don't know how I got to this point. I just lived through things until daily life seemed less painful. It just seemed to happen. I only know I have changed."

FAITH: A SURE FOUNDATION

I can do all things through Christ who strengthens me.
Philippians 4:13, New King James Bible

Contentment is anchored in a faith that has withstood the tests of life's trage-dies and triumphs. Faith provides peace and a space in which insights and self-understanding can breed wisdom and fortitude for a future ripe with possibilities. Contentment can be the reward of grief faced and tamed.

Often, when enough time has passed, a woman can look back over her experi-ence of widowhood and realize the many ways God's presence and love have been a sustaining force in her life. A sense of self-confidence takes root when she claims the basic fact that the God of her past will continue to be the God of her future, thus fear and anxiety give way to courage and peace.

The unanswerable questions of life and death are now accepted as divine mys-teries yet to be made known. However, a deepening perception of reconciliation and resurrection has staved off unsettling doubt.

Many widows have reached this point with the support of a loving church family. Others have found greatest spiritual help from a specific mentor or spiri-tual friend. Undoubtedly, a solid bedrock of faith is best achieved through the discipline of regular worship, Bible study, and prayer.

When a widow has acknowledged and received God's love and direction in her life, she is better able to make a variety of choices which may lead to a new career, unexpected relationships, or life in a different location. However, she does not have to make hurried decisions, because she is sustained by a hard-won life of contentment grounded in a mature faith

Life will never be void of sadness and struggle, but life can be savored with gifts of faith, joy, peace, and happiness.

BEDROCK OF SCRIPTURE

Let love be genuine; hate what is evil, hold fast to what is good; love one another with mutual affection; outdo one another in showing honor. Do not lag in zeal, be ardent in spirit, serve the Lord. Rejoice in hope, be patient in suffering, persevere in prayer. Contribute to the needs of the saints; extend hospitality to strangers.

Bless those who persecute you; bless and do not curse them. Rejoice with those who rejoice, weep with those who weep. Live in harmony with one another; do not be haughty, but associate with the lowly; do not claim to be wiser than you are. Do not repay anyone evil for evil, but take thought for what is noble in the sight of all. If it is possible, so far as it depends on you, live peaceably with all. Romans 12:9-18

Peace I leave with you; my peace I give to you. I do not give to you as the world gives. Do not let your hearts be troubled, and do not let them be afraid. John 14:27

I lift up my eyes to the hills—
from where will my help come?
My help comes from the Lord,
who made heaven and earth.
He will not let your foot be moved;
he who keeps you will not slumber.
He who keeps Israel
will neither slumber nor sleep.
The Lord is your keeper;
the Lord is your shade at your right hand.
The sun shall not strike you by day,
nor the moon by night.
The Lord will keep you from all evil;

he will keep your life.
The Lord will keep
your going out and your coming in
from this time on and forevermore. Psalm 121

Then they cried to the Lord in their trouble,
and he brought them out from their distress;
he made the storm be still,
and the waves of the sea were hushed.
Then they were glad because they had quiet,
and he brought them to their desired haven.
Let them thank the Lord for his steadfast love,
for his wonderful works to humankind.
Let them extol him in the congregation of the people,
and praise him in the assembly of the elders. Psalm 107:28-32

PRAYER OF CONTENTMENT

At last, prayer is an offering from the heart!

Ever-loving God, a long time ago someone told me that life is an invitation to a journey through the wilderness, sustained by Your love and grace. Widowhood is that kind of journey—full of pain, confusion, and questions; but You pulled me through those awful days. At long last, I now am satisfied with the peace and the pace of my life.

Once when I had the flu, I thought I was dying. Then one morning I awoke without chills or fever. I suddenly knew that I was getting well. I felt like a miracle had touched me. That's the way I feel now!

I never thought I could be this strong, but it was out of my utter weakness that I came to trust You for all my tomorrows. The chills and aches of grief have been replaced with the growing certainty that life has meaning, and I have a place in the present, as well as in time yet to come. I am comfortable with questions that defy answers and dreams that may never take form and substance. Out of the chaos of my life, Your presence has led me to peace.

I am thankful for special friends and my precious family who allowed me to be weak, while they remained strong. I have received so much from so many people; help me to know how to give back to others who find their lives shattered into a million pieces. I do not have a large vocabulary of faith, but I do know the movements of faith: to reach out for hands to hold in the dark night of the soul; to sit still and know that You are God; to reach deep inside to share with others the compassion that has been wrapped around me.

I want to shout from the housetops! I am not afraid or angry any more God, You are with me! Hallelujah and Amen!

I-CAN COVENANT

I can be joyful as a new person.
I can do what I have to do.
I can survive.
I can grow.
I can do difficult things.
I can plan for the future.
I can set new goals and achieve them.
I can ask others for help.
I can cry, or not cry, as I please.
I can make new friends.
I can have great self-confidence.
I can defeat my worst fears.
I can live alone successfully.
I can celebrate my life as it is now.
I can live my life in contentment.
I can praise God for God's love and grace.
I can thank God for God's sustaining presence.

ADDENDUM

PEACE OF MIND
FINANCIAL MANAGEMENT FOR LIFE

By Julie Yarbrough
Julie Yarbrough Financial Consulting, LLC
Dallas, Texas

TAKE CARE OF YOURSELF:
TWENTY THINGS YOU SHOULD KNOW ABOUT STAYING
HEALTHY

By Dr. Gretchen Toler, MD
Cooper Clinic, Dallas, Texas

PEACE OF MIND
FINANCIAL MANAGEMENT FOR LIFE

At any time in life, financial management can seem like an overwhelming task, but it may become a daunting challenge at the time of grief. One of the most fearful things that we face after death is financial management. Although there are no quick or easy progressions through the *emotional* stages of grief, finances and money management are *business*, and do not merit an investment of the precious emotional energy that can and should be directed to issues of the heart, mind, and spirit.

No one cares about your money like you care about your money. Trusted advisors, children, and those in the financial services industry generally are not personally invested in your financial health and well-being. No one should rely entirely on others for important financial management decisions unless *physically or mentally unable* to function or cope. *Not knowing* is a major contributor to fear, something that comes in abundant supply with grief. Peace of mind results from addressing the many issues of financial management realistically and proactively. A sense of personal confidence and serenity about the stewardship of earthly resources is a gift to yourself and to those you love.

Used by permission from *Peace of Mind—Financial Management for Life* © 2005 by Julie Yarbrough, Julie Yarbrough Financial Consulting, LLC, yinvest@sbcglobal.net.

ACTION PLAN

The ACTION PLAN is a reminder of information that is important at any time, but especially at the time of death.

- REVIEW YOUR PERSONAL DOCUMENTS AND REVISE AS NEEDED.
    - Statutory Durable Power of Attorney
    - Medical Power of Attorney
    - Living Will/Directives to Physicians
    - Last Will and Testament
    - Trust Agreements
    - Burial Arrangements/Funeral Plans/Obituary Notice

- CONTACT THE SOCIAL SECURITY ADMINISTRATION.
    - Report the death.
    - Request the necessary changes for survivor benefit payments.
    - Apply for the one-time death benefit ($255.00).
    - Request direct deposit of social security benefits to designated bank account.

- WORK WITH YOUR CPA AND ATTORNEY TO FILE:
    - Estate Tax Return—due 9 months after date of death
    - Federal and State Tax Returns

- OTHER CONTACTS:
    - Insurance Companies
        - Request claims forms.
        - File for benefits.

- Request form 712 for insurance claims paid for Estate Tax Return.

- Banks/Credit Unions

  - Report the death.

  - Check for insurance coverage on loans.

- Current and Former Employers

  - Report the death.

  - Check for potential benefits—group insurance, pension, etc.

- Professional, fraternal, other associations

  - Report the death.

  - Cancel publications.

  - Request refund of unused dues.

  - Check for assistance or benefits.

- Department of Veterans Affairs in the case of military service.

- REVIEW YOUR LIFE INSURANCE, PROPERTY INSURANCE, AUTO INSURANCE, AND LIABILITY INSURANCE COVERAGE.

  - Make sure that the ownership of the policy is correct and current.

  - Make sure that the beneficiary designations are current.

- CONSULT WITH A TAX PROFESSIONAL BEFORE MAKING DECISIONS REGARDING:

  - JOINT ACCOUNTS

  - TITLES AND DEEDS TO VEHICLES AND/OR REAL ESTATE

  - RETIREMENT AND INVESTMENT ACCOUNTS

OWNERSHIP CHANGES AND ASSET TRANSFERS CAN HAVE
TAX IMPLICATIONS THAT CAN BEST BE EVALUATED BY A
TAX PROFESSIONAL OR ATTORNEY.

- AN EXTREMELY IMPORTANT AREA OF FINANCIAL VULNERA-
  BILITY IS CREDIT CARDS.

  - Pay off and cancel any individual store credit cards; commit to the
    use of one major credit card for most purchases made with a credit
    card.

  - Consolidate into one card any multiple card accounts (American
    Express, MasterCard, Visa).

  - Change the name of the cardholder on the account for credit cards
    to your name as the primary and sole card holder.

  - If your card gives travel or other awards for dollars spent, make
    sure that your linked airline miles program (AAdvantage, Delta
    SkyMiles, etc.) is the one receiving the credit.

  - Inquire about any possible life insurance or accidental death life
    insurance benefits that may be payable through the credit card
    company.

- REQUEST A COPY OF YOUR CREDIT REPORT FROM ONE OF THE MAJOR CREDIT REPORTING COMPANIES (Equifax, Experian, TransUnion). THESE CAN BE OBTAINED ON-LINE, OR ORDERED BY TELEPHONE.

  - Make sure that the Credit Reporting Companies are aware that there has been a death and that the social security number is not being fraudulently used.

  - You might want to consider signing up and paying for (approximate cost $100 per year) a credit watch service. This can be applied for with any of the credit reporting companies; you receive immediate notification if there are any irregularities on any credit accounts or unusual activity using your name or social security number.

- FINALLY, THINK ABOUT THE "BELT AND SUSPENDERS" APPROACH TO MATTERS OF YOUR OWN PERSONAL SAFETY.

  - DO YOU HAVE A HOME FIRE EXTINGUISHER?

    - WHERE IS IT?

    - HOW OLD IS IT?

    - DO YOU KNOW HOW TO USE IT?

    - IS IT THE RIGHT EXTINGUISHER FOR THE AREA OF THE HOUSE IN WHICH IT IS PLACED?

      - There are different types of extinguishers for different types of fire—electrical, chemical, cooking fires, etc. Some are multi-purpose extinguishers.

      - Make sure that you have one that is accessible and not too bulky. They come in a variety of sizes and are not difficult to use; the smaller ones cost about $10.00 each. You might want to have one for the kitchen, the laundry room/area, the garage, and/or your bedroom for additional peace of mind.

  - DOES YOUR HOUSE HAVE A SMOKE DETECTOR/ALARM?

    - IS IT BATTERY-POWERED?

    - DO YOU HAVE A REGULAR SCHEDULE FOR CHANGING THE BATTERIES?

- DO YOU HAVE A 24-HOUR PHARMACY?

  - DO YOU KNOW THE TELEPHONE NUMBER?

  - DO THEY DELIVER?

  - IS THERE A DRIVE-THROUGH WINDOW FOR PICK-UP?

  - ARE YOU REGISTERED THERE IF YOUR PHYSICIAN NEEDS TO CALL IN A PRESCRIPTION FOR YOU DURING THE NIGHT?

  - EVEN IF THIS IS NOT YOUR REGULAR PHARMACY, IT IS STILL POSSIBLE TO REGISTER AND BE "ON FILE" IN THE EVENT OF AN AFTER-HOURS NEED.

- DO YOU HAVE A MEDICAL CONDITION FOR WHICH YOU SHOULD WEAR A MEDIC ALERT BRACELET?

- IF YOU LIVE ALONE, SHOULD YOU CONSIDER HAVING LIFE ALERT OR A SIMILAR PERSONAL IN-HOME MONITORING SYSTEM?

- DO YOU HAVE AN EXTENDED WARRANTY ON YOUR CAR IF YOU DRIVE AN OLDER MODEL AND PLAN TO KEEP IT FOR AN ADDITIONAL PERIOD OF TIME?

    - IS A ROADSIDE ASSISTANCE SERVICE READILY AVAILABLE TO YOU?

        - THROUGH AAA, YOUR EXTENDED WARRANTY PLAN, AUTOMOBILE DEALERSHIP, ONSTAR?

        - DO YOU HAVE WITH YOU IN THE CAR AND KNOW HOW TO USE A CELLULAR PHONE IN THE EVENT OF AN EMERGENCY OR NEED?

- DO YOU HAVE A SERVICE WARRANTY FOR THE APPLIANCES IN YOUR HOME?

    - THIS IS NOT THE SAME AS THE MANUFACTURER'S WARRANTY GIVEN WHEN THE APPLIANCE WAS NEW.

    - THIS SERVICE WARRANTY (BASIC ANNUAL COST AROUND $350-450) COVERS SERVICE CALLS AND REPAIRS TO APPLIANCES WHICH CAN BE EXTREMELY EXPENSIVE AND RESULT IN UNANTICIPATED AND PERHAPS UNBUDGETED COSTS.

LOCATION OF IMPORTANT DOCUMENTS AND PAPERS

NAME OF DOCUMENT/RECORD   LOCATION

HEALTH HISTORY INFORMATION

LIVING WILL (HIPAA COMPLIANT)

DIRECTIVE TO PHYSICIANS

DNR (DO NOT RESUSCITATE) DIRECTIVE
    IN HOSPITAL/FACILITY
    AT HOME

ORGAN DONOR DIRECTIVE

DURABLE POWER OF ATTORNEY FOR HEALTH CARE

DEED TO CEMETERY LOT

FUNERAL INSTRUCTIONS

OBITUARY NOTICE

PRE-NEED FUNERAL ARRANGEMENTS DOCUMENTS

MILITARY SERVICE RECORDS

CITIZENSHIP PAPERS

BAPTISMAL OR CONFIRMATION CERTIFICATES

BIRTH CERTIFICATES/ADOPTION PAPERS

MARRIAGE LICENSE

DIVORCE DOCUMENTS

LAST WILL AND TESTAMENT _____

TRUST DOCUMENTS _____

SAFE DEPOSIT BOX KEYS _____

OTHER IMPORTANT KEYS _____

DEATH CERTIFICATES _____

PASSPORTS _____

BUSINESS DOCUMENTS:

   STATUTORY DURABLE POWER OF ATTORNEY _____

   CHECK BOOKS _____

   SAVINGS BOOKS _____

   INSTALLMENT MORTGAGE/LOAN PAYMENT BOOKS ____

   CREDIT CARDS/ID CARDS _____

   CREDIT REPORT _____

   EMPLOYMENT INCOME RECORDS _____

   BANK STATEMENTS/CANCELLED CHECKS _____

   BROKERAGE/INVESTMENT STATEMENTS _____

   STOCK/BOND CERTIFICATES _____

   SOCIAL SECURITY STATEMENTS _____

   PENSION PLAN STATEMENTS _____

RETIREMENT PLAN (IRA, ETC.) STATEMENTS

INSURANCE POLICIES:

LONG TERM CARE

ACCIDENT/DISABILITY

HEALTH

LIFE

PROPERTY

AUTOMOBILE

LIABILITY

REAL ESTATE DOCUMENTS:

TITLE/DEED TO HOME

TITLE/DEED TO OTHER REAL PROPERTY

MORTGAGE DOCUMENTS

PROPERTY RECORDS (LEASES, LIENS, ETC.)

WARRANTIES/GUARANTEES

AUTOMOBILE DOCUMENTS:

AUTOMOBILE TITLE

<u>BILL OF SALE/LEASE AGREEMENT</u> _____

<u>REGISTRATION INFORMATION</u> _____

<u>TAX INFORMATION:</u>

<u>PREVIOUS YEARS' TAX RETURNS</u> _____

<u>PROPERTY INVENTORY/APPRAISALS</u> _____

<u>RECEIPTS</u> _____

<u>RECEIPTS FROM ESTATE ADMINISTRATION EXPENSES</u> _____

<u>COMPUTER PROGRAMS:</u>

<u>COMPUTER LOGIN</u>   <u>PASSWORD</u>

<u>PROGRAM</u>   <u>USER ID</u>   <u>PASSWORD</u>

<u>PROGRAM</u>   <u>USER ID</u>   <u>PASSWORD</u>

<u>PROGRAM</u>   <u>USER ID</u>   <u>PASSWORD</u>

PERSONAL FINANCIAL INVENTORY

ASSETS

CHECKING ACCOUNT(S) $

SAVINGS ACCOUNT(S) $

CERTIFICATES OF DEPOSIT $

MONEY MARKET FUNDS $

INVESTMENTS:
    STOCKS $
    BONDS $
    MUTUAL FUNDS $

IRA $

ANNUITIES $

LIFE INSURANCE AND DEATH BENEFITS $

COMPANY BENEFITS:
    STOCK OPTIONS $
    SAVINGS/401(k) PLANS $
    ESOP/PAYSOP $

PENSION PLAN $

DEFERRED COMPENSATION $

REAL ESTATE:

HOMESTEAD $

SECOND HOME $

RENTAL PROPERTIES $

MORTGAGES/DEEDS RECEIVABLE $

REAL PROPERTY:

OIL AND GAS INTERESTS $

PARTNERSHIP INTERESTS $

PERSONAL PROPERTY:

FINE ART $

JEWELRY $

HOUSEHOLD FURNISHINGS $

AUTOMOBILES $

OTHER PERSONAL EFFECTS $

ESTIMATE OF TOTAL ASSETS $

PERSONAL MONTHLY MANAGEMENT BUDGET

INCOME:

SALARY/WAGES/COMPENSATION	$
SOCIAL SECURITY	$
IRA	$
ANNUITY	$
PENSION PLAN	$
INVESTMENT INCOME	$
ESTIMATE OF TOTAL MONTHLY INCOME	$
ESTIMATE OF TOTAL ANNUAL INCOME	$

EXPENSES:

HOUSING:

RENT/MORTGAGE	$
ASSOCIATION FEES OR DUES	$
INSURANCE	$
TAXES	$
HOME MAINTENANCE	$

UTILITIES:

GAS	$
ELECTRICITY	$
WATER	$
TELEPHONE	$
CABLE/INTERNET SERVICE	$

FOOD $

MEDICAL $

WORK-RELATED EXPENSES $

TRANSPORTATION:
   AUTOMOBILE LOAN PAYMENT $
   GAS/MAINTENANCE $
   INSURANCE $

PENSION/401(k) $

IRA $

SAVINGS $

SUPPORT OF DEPENDENT(S) $

TAXES $

CONTRIBUTIONS $

INSURANCE:
   LIFE INSURANCE $
   HEALTH INSURANCE $
   LONG TERM CARE INSURANCE $

PERSONAL EXPENSES:

    CLOTHING   **$**

    ENTERTAINMENT   **$**

    TRAVEL   **$**

    EDUCATION   **$**

    GIFTS   **$**

    PERSONAL ITEMS   **$**

ESTIMATE OF TOTAL MONTHLY EXPENSES   **$**

ESTIMATE OF TOTAL ANNUAL EXPENSES   **$**

TAKING CARE OF YOURSELF TWENTY THINGS YOU SHOULD KNOW ABOUT STAYING HEALTHY

For all ages:

1.   <u>Exercise is not optional</u>. Aim for 30 minutes of moderate activity (such as brisk walking) daily to improve fitness and help to fight depression. Light weight training two to three times weekly improves muscle tone and bone strength. If you are just starting an exercise program, talk to your doctor.

2.   <u>Eat a healthy diet</u>. Aim for at least five servings of fruits and vegetables per day. Get omega 3 fatty acids in your diet (from salmon or flax seed). Get rid of the refined sugar, fast food, and junk.

3.   <u>Drink plenty of water</u>. This improve energy, skin tone and kidney function.

4.   <u>Take at least a multivitamin daily</u>. Talk to your doctor about whether you should take omega 3 fatty acids, calcium supplements, and extra antioxidants.

5.   <u>Quit smoking</u>. You may double your risk of a heart attack with even two cigarettes per day.

6.   <u>Moderate alcohol and do not take recreational drugs</u>. These substances are lousy choices for medicating depression, anxiety, and insomnia. If you feel you are dependent on alcohol or drugs, get help quickly. As a general rule, women should limit alcohol to six servings per week (not all at one time!). Women with certain medical conditions (including high blood pressure, osteoporosis, depression, high triglycerides. or liver disease) should limit alcohol intake even more. If you are not sure, talk to your doctor.

7.   <u>Ease up on the caffeine</u>. You don't need another reason to lose sleep or feel anxious. Limit yourself to one or two servings early in the day.

8. <u>Be sensible about safety</u>. Sturdy locks, a good security system, a smoke alarm, a fire extinguisher, a cell phone, a dog, and a little common sense are helpful. If you go out alone, make sure someone knows where you are and how to reach you. Keep emergency contact numbers in your purse and by your phone.

9. <u>Fight off infection</u>. Wash your hands before eating. Keep alcohol hand sanitizer in your purse. Get your immunizations updated.

10. <u>Brush and floss</u>. Poor dental hygiene can lead to malnutrition, heart disease and infection. Make an appointment with your dentist.

11. <u>Get a medical checkup</u>. Know your risks for cardiovascular disease, diabetes, and osteoporosis. These are preventable conditions that can cause serious health problems later in life. Get regular gynecological exams and skin exams.

12. <u>Review all your medications</u> (including over the counter and herbal preparations) with your doctor. Throw away any medications you are no longer taking. Take the ones you are supposed to be taking as directed. Keep a list of medications in your purse.

13. <u>Screening tests can save lives</u>. Pap smears every one to three years, yearly mammograms after 40, colonoscopy after 50, bone density screening for osteoporosis, a stress test...talk to your doctor about the tests that are appropriate for you.

14. If you choose to be <u>sexually active</u>, make sure you and your partner get screening for sexually transmitted diseases. Condoms help, but they are not 100% effective. Unless you are ready to get pregnant, talk to your doctor about birth control options.

15. <u>Put your wishes in writing</u>. Have a lawyer help you prepare a living will, and a durable power of attorney for healthcare. You are never too young to make these decisions.

    As you get older:

16. <u>Don't fall</u>. A hip fracture could land you in a nursing home permanently. Get screening for osteoporosis. Use night-lights and support rails in the

bathroom. Get rid of throw rugs. Swallow your pride and get some sensible shoes, for goodness sake.

17.   Don't ignore persistent muscle and joint pain. These can lead to loss of function and disability. Talk to your doctor.

18.   Get over your embarrassment. Tell your doctor about dizziness, memory loss, hearing loss, poor vision, and bladder or bowel problems. These problems are often treatable.

19.   Have a buddy system. Check in with someone daily.

20.   Plan for the future. You may have to leave your home eventually. Have a frank discussion with your family about your wishes.

Gretchen Toler, MD
Cooper Clinic, Dallas Texas

About the Author

Patsy Brundige is a journalist and United Methodist Pastor who has led countless widows through grief experiences. Pat Millican is a book reviewer and researcher. Both women are widows.

978-0-595-27460-4
0-595-27460-9

CPSIA information can be obtained
at www.ICGtesting.com
Printed in the USA
BVHW031746130721
611856BV00001B/9

9 780595 274604